METACOGNITIVE
TEACHING

Metacognitive Teaching

How to narrow the attainment gap and promote equity in the classroom

Anoara Mughal

BLOOMSBURY EDUCATION

LONDON OXFORD NEW YORK NEW DELHI SYDNEY

BLOOMSBURY EDUCATION
Bloomsbury Publishing Plc
50 Bedford Square, London WC1B 3DP, UK
Bloomsbury Publishing Ireland Limited
29 Earlsfort Terrace, Dublin 2, D02 AY28, Ireland

BLOOMSBURY, BLOOMSBURY EDUCATION and the
Diana logo are trademarks of Bloomsbury Publishing Plc

First published in the United Kingdom in 2026 by Bloomsbury Publishing Plc

This edition published in the United Kingdom in 2026 by Bloomsbury Publishing Plc

A catalogue record for this book is available from the British Library

ISBN: PB: 978-1-80199-814-7; ePub: 978-1-80199-816-1

2 4 6 8 10 9 7 5 3 1

Cover design by Adam Renvoize

Typeset by Lumina Datamatics Ltd
Printed and bound in Great Britain by TJ Books, Padstow, Cornwall

To find out more about our authors and books visit www.bloomsbury.com
and sign up for our newsletters
For product safety related questions contact productsafety@bloomsbury.com

Acknowledgements

Writing can feel like a solitary process; each sentence shaped in the silent space of thought. Yet it transforms when supported by catalysts – trusted readers, mentors or collaborators – who offer clarity, encouragement and perspective.

Their presence doesn't erase solitude, but it steadies the work, helping ideas align and finally come together into a finished piece that beautifully reflects shared strength. Because their guidance transforms solitary effort into work that carries far greater strength, clarity and purpose, it feels only right to acknowledge and thank the people who made that journey possible.

Firstly, the editorial team at Bloomsbury. Emily Evans and Lucy Vallance, commissioning editors, and Holly Edgar, my senior editor, enabled this book to be written. Emily Evans and Lucy Vallance for their initial involvement in the book; Lucy Vallance for nudging me on the proposals and the conversations that helped shape this book. Holly Edgar, thank you for your patience and faith in me as a writer, for bringing the book to life and for (thankfully) minimal edits to the manuscript.

The WomenEd team, for their support and encouragement, in particular Vivienne Porrit, Christalla Jamil, Hannah Wilson and Dr Jennifer A Hawkins.

The team at Healthy Toolkit, who have always supported and championed my work: Andrew Cowley, Helen Damini, Cherryl Drabble, Samira Ashraf, Rae Snape, Matt Young, Adrian Bethune, and Jackie Ward.

To all the mentors and coaches on and off social media I have had throughout my career; thank you for giving me the support and confidence to truly believe in myself and thrive.

None of this would have been possible without the love and support of my family: my parents, Banecha Khatun and Shona Miah; my husband Arif; my sons Zuhayr and Zain; and my daughter Sara, who have grown accustomed to the constant sound of typing. Thank you for your patience, encouragement and for always taking care of me.

Contents

1 Understanding disadvantage and barriers to learning

Introduction

In today's educational landscape, supporting disadvantaged pupils is essential. These learners often face systemic barriers – economic, social, cultural or geographic – that limit access to resources and opportunities, contributing to persistent achievement gaps (Department for Education, 2024). In England, eligibility for free school meals is one indicator of disadvantage, but disadvantage also encompasses family instability, limited educational support and high-deprivation areas, and learners with special educational needs and disabilities (SEND), according to the Education Endowment Foundation (EEF, 2020).

Neurodivergent[1] pupils, including those with Attention Deficit Hyperactivity Disorder (ADHD), dyslexia or autism, encounter additional challenges that affect attention, memory, executive function, social communication and sensory processing. SEND covers a wide range of learning needs and disabilities, including many that are not related to neurodivergence. Some neurodivergent learners may need support through the SEND system, but not all, and not all learners with SEND are neurodivergent. Many disadvantaged pupils may also be neurodivergent, and may be learners with SEND, creating overlapping challenges.

It is important to distinguish between neurodivergent learners and learners with SEND. In the UK context, a child or young person is said to have SEND if they have:

- a learning difficulty or a disability that means they require special educational provision (GOV.UK, n.d.)
- a significantly greater difficulty in learning than most children of the same age, or a disability that prevents or hinders them from using facilities that are generally available to their peers.

---

[1]'Neurodivergent' refers to people whose cognitive processing differs from what is considered typical.

Special educational provision refers to support that is additional to or different from what is normally provided (BEA Service, n.d.).

Disability, in this context, is defined under the Equality Act 2010 as a physical or mental impairment with a long-term and substantial adverse effect on day-to-day activities (beaservice.org.uk).

Finally, the four broad areas of need that SEND provision commonly covers are:

- communication and interaction
- cognition and learning
- social, emotional and mental health
- sensory and/or physical needs.

Traditional teaching methods – such as uniform pacing, lecture-based instruction and abstract tasks – often fail to meet the needs of these pupils. Without scaffolding, differentiation or multimodal learning opportunities, learners may experience repeated failure, disengagement and low motivation.

Fostering metacognition – the awareness and control of one's own learning processes – offers a practical solution. When educators integrate explicit instruction, inquiry-based learning and reflection strategies into their teaching practices, pupils can develop self-regulation, problem-solving skills and adaptive learning strategies. Interventions that combine academic content with metacognitive skill development help students leverage strengths, compensate for challenges and navigate educational inequities.

This chapter examines the specific barriers disadvantaged students face, explores why traditional interventions fall short, and introduces metacognition as a transformative approach. Chapter 2 will then provide the theoretical foundation for understanding how metacognition works and why it is particularly powerful for disadvantaged learners.

Educational outcomes and attainment gaps

Disadvantaged and disabled students consistently achieve lower outcomes than their peers. In England, the attainment gap emerges early and widens over time. According to the Education Policy Institute (2024), five-year-olds with SEND are now 20.1 months behind their peers – an alarming indicator of a worsening educational crisis five years on from the COVID-19 pandemic.

Persistent disparities in attainment are evident across all stages of education. The Nuffield Foundation (2025) reports that pupils eligible for free school meals are less likely to reach a 'good level of development' at age five and consistently underperform at GCSEs, particularly in English and mathematics. These gaps extend into post-16 education, where disadvantaged students are underrepresented in higher education and high-quality vocational pathways.

Disadvantaged pupils are affected by a complex interplay of socioeconomic, environmental, personal and psychological factors. Material deprivation, limited academic support at home, low self-efficacy and mental health challenges interact to reinforce educational gaps. Evidence from the Institute for Government, Nuffield Foundation (2025), and the Institute for Fiscal Studies (IFS) underscores the need for interventions that address both academic support and the development of resilience and self-regulation.

Barriers to learning

Disadvantaged pupils face multiple, overlapping barriers that affect both immediate learning and long-term outcomes. These challenges are structural, socioeconomic, environmental, personal and psychological.

Socioeconomic challenges

Socioeconomic disadvantage remains a major obstacle to learning. Children from low-income households often lack access to books, digital devices, tutoring and enrichment activities that support literacy and numeracy. As noted earlier, pupils eligible for free school meals consistently achieve lower outcomes compared to peers across all educational stages, including Key Stage assessments and GCSEs.

Material deprivation often intersects with social pressures: families may live in overcrowded or unstable housing, or in neighbourhoods with limited educational resources, which restricts access to informal learning opportunities. Economic stress can also undermine emotional wellbeing, diminishing focus, engagement and cognitive development.

In the classroom, the effects of poverty are often visible to teachers, yet rarely spoken about. A pupil may arrive without having completed their homework – not due to a lack of motivation, but because they spent the previous evening in a hostel following an eviction, with no quiet place to study and no adult available to help them. Another pupil's persistent absences may not reflect truancy, but rather caring responsibilities such as looking after younger siblings while a single parent works multiple jobs. Similarly, a student's reluctance to participate in discussions may stem from anxiety about not having 'the right words', often a consequence of limited exposure to the more sophisticated language patterns their wealthier peers acquire through dinner-table conversations, museum visits and bedtime reading (Lareau, 2003). These are not isolated incidents but everyday realities for many disadvantaged pupils, creating a cumulative burden that significantly affects their ability to engage with learning.

Environmental challenges

Home environments can limit pupils' engagement with schoolwork. Those living in overcrowded or insecure housing often lack quiet, stable spaces for study and rest. Disadvantaged pupils frequently encounter difficulties with homework, time management and access to enrichment activities that foster critical thinking, relying heavily on schools to compensate for limited support at home (Nuffield Foundation, 2025). These stressors can contribute to fatigue, anxiety and difficulty concentrating in class.

Seminal research by Hart and Risley (1995) revealed dramatic differences in the amount and type of language children experience in their early years. Children from professional families heard approximately 30 million more words by age four than children from families on benefits. Crucially, this wasn't just about quantity; it was about the types of interactions that build academic discourse patterns.

This research reveals why some students arrive at school already familiar with the kind of questioning, elaborated explanations and abstract thinking that characterises academic discourse, while others have had limited exposure to these patterns. Students from the second group aren't lacking in intelligence or capability; they simply haven't had the same opportunities to develop familiarity with school-based communication styles.

Personal and psychological factors

Mental health issues, often exacerbated by socioeconomic stressors, are widespread among disadvantaged pupils. These pupils are more likely to experience behavioural and emotional disorders yet frequently face barriers to accessing appropriate support (Costello et al., 2003; Reiss, 2013). Chronic stress impairs concentration, memory, impulse control and problem-solving, undermining both engagement and academic performance (Evans & Kim, 2013; Lupien et al., 2009).

These psychological barriers often manifest in familiar classroom behaviours. A Year 6 pupil might declare 'I can't do this' before even reading a maths problem, or refuse to attempt creative writing, insisting 'I'm rubbish at English.' Such statements aren't accurate self-assessments but protective strategies developed in response to repeated academic setbacks. The pupil has learned that not trying feels safer than trying and failing again – a phenomenon known as 'learned helplessness' (Seligman, 1972).

Low self-efficacy – the belief in one's capacity to succeed – further compounds these difficulties. When pupils consistently see their more privileged peers outperforming them, and lack role models who have overcome similar barriers, they may internalise the belief that academic success is not for 'people like them' (Bandura, 1997). This becomes a self-fulfilling prophecy: repeated setbacks at school and at home erode confidence, leading to avoidance of challenging tasks, reluctance to participate and reduced persistence. Stress, anxiety and behavioural difficulties intensify these challenges, contributing to absenteeism and diminished learning capacity (IFS, 2024).

Cultural and linguistic diversity

Disadvantaged pupils from minoritised ethnic backgrounds often face compounded barriers that intersect with socioeconomic disadvantage. Pupils for whom English is an additional language may struggle to access curriculum content not because of limited cognitive ability, but because they're simultaneously learning academic content and the language of instruction (Strand & Demie, 2005). A Year 7 science pupil might fully grasp the concept of photosynthesis but lack the English vocabulary required to express their understanding in written assessments.

Cultural differences in communication styles and learning approaches may be misinterpreted as disengagement or lack of understanding. Research by Heath (1983) demonstrated that working-class and minoritised communities often use different narrative structures and questioning patterns than those from more privileged communities. When a teacher asks 'What might happen if...?', they're using a hypothetical questioning style common in middle-class homes but potentially unfamiliar to pupils from other backgrounds. These pupils may possess rich knowledge and sophisticated thinking but lack familiarity with the particular discourse patterns valued in educational settings.

Teachers can unconsciously hold lower expectations for pupils from particular ethnic backgrounds, influenced by broader societal stereotypes about academic ability (Gillborn, 2008; Strand, 2014). The intersection of ethnicity and socioeconomic disadvantage creates particularly acute barriers: pupils who are both from low-income households and from minoritised communities face multiple layers of structural inequality that compound one another.

Behaviour, motivation and resilience

Behavioural difficulties, such as conduct problems or withdrawing socially, frequently go hand in hand with low motivation. These students may perceive education as irrelevant or unattainable, which can reduce engagement and participation (IFS, 2024). Resilience is not uniform: while some pupils develop coping strategies when supported, others internalise failure, becoming risk-averse and limiting their own skill development. Consistent encouragement, clear guidance and positive role models can make a significant difference, increasing the likelihood that pupils will persevere academically.

Reduced motivation might present as a Year 8 pupil consistently sitting at the back, hood up, refusing to engage – not because they don't care about learning, but because school has repeatedly confirmed their belief that academic success isn't 'for people like them' (Gorard & See, 2013). What may appear as disengagement is often a rational response to repeated failure despite genuine effort. But not all disadvantaged pupils respond the same way. Some demonstrate remarkable resilience, drawing strength from family values, community support or personal determination to overcome obstacles. Recognising this variation is crucial: identical circumstances do not produce identical responses. Individual agency and supportive relationships play a vital role in shaping outcomes.

Parental engagement and resource gaps

Parents in low-income households often work long hours or multiple jobs, limiting the time they have available to support learning. Disadvantaged pupils frequently lack access to books, technology, quiet study spaces and enrichment activities – constraining intellectual growth (Sutton Trust, 2021).

Parental attitudes and expectations also shape outcomes. Financial and health pressures may restrict involvement, while more advantaged households often provide guidance, monitor progress and maintain high expectations. Limited parental education further reduces the capacity to support learning, making it harder to assist with homework or foster higher-order thinking skills (IFS, 2020).

Cumulative impact on learning

Limited guidance, restricted resources and reduced parental engagement create cumulative disadvantage. Disadvantaged pupils often rely almost entirely on school for learning, making classroom instruction their primary source of academic development. When school support alone cannot close learning gaps, these pupils fall further behind peers who benefit from support both at home and in school. Addressing these disparities requires strategies that extend learning beyond the classroom, including targeted homework support, access to resources and initiatives to engage parents.

While increased funding and curriculum reforms are important, they are not enough on their own to close the attainment gap. Research shows that traditional interventions often fail to address the multifaceted nature of disadvantage. Curriculum reforms often overlook personalised approaches, while teacher-centred methods and standardised assessments fail to engage students or develop critical thinking, problem-solving and crucial skills such as resilience, self-regulation and motivation. For disadvantaged pupils facing low self-efficacy and limited home support, we need targeted interventions in order to reduce educational inequalities effectively.

Long-term educational impact

The interplay of low self-efficacy, mental health difficulties, behavioural challenges and reduced motivation has lasting consequences for educational trajectories. Disadvantaged pupils are less likely to complete secondary education with strong outcomes, less likely to progress to higher education, and more likely to face limited career prospects. Addressing these personal and psychological barriers is essential to promoting equity and enabling pupils to realise their potential.

These long-term consequences do not emerge in isolation; they are closely tied to the everyday learning environments that shape pupils' habits and expectations long before key educational decisions are made. The same psychological and motivational barriers that influence attainment also affect how pupils experience learning on a day-to-day basis – how confident they feel approaching tasks, how independently they work and how consistently they engage with schoolwork outside the classroom. It is within this context that differences in home learning environments become especially significant, as they can either reinforce existing challenges or provide the scaffolding pupils need to overcome them.

Differences in learning experiences

These cumulative disadvantages create clear differences in the academic support disadvantaged pupils receive at home. Academic support includes the help pupils receive to engage with schoolwork, complete assignments and develop effective learning habits. For many disadvantaged pupils, this support is limited due to a combination of socioeconomic, cultural and structural factors.

In the classroom, these differences often surface in the way pupils approach learning. Some may hesitate to begin tasks on their own, wait for direct instruction instead of taking initiative or abandon a task quickly when it becomes challenging. This isn't a reflection of ability; rather, it highlights a lack of exposure to the self-regulatory strategies that many of their more advantaged peers acquire at home through modelled problem-solving and guided practice (Sylva et al., 2004).

A similar pattern can be seen in pupils' confidence. Those who have repeatedly encountered barriers to learning may feel unsure about asking questions or seeking support, sometimes believing they should already know how to tackle unfamiliar work. Meanwhile, pupils from more advantaged backgrounds often come to school already familiar with core learning behaviours – breaking tasks into manageable steps, checking their work or asking for clarification – because these skills have been explicitly taught, encouraged and normalised at home (Hart & Risley, 1995).

Barriers for disabled disadvantaged students

Disadvantaged pupils with disabilities face unique obstacles that can significantly impede their educational progress:

* Limited access to resources: These pupils often lack specialised learning materials, assistive technologies and individualised support – resources that are crucial for equitable academic development.

- Environmental stressors: Unstable housing, food insecurity and high-stress living conditions negatively affect cognitive functions such as attention, memory and executive functioning.

- Systemic inequities: Schools in under-resourced areas may lack trained staff, appropriate accommodations and inclusive curricula, compounding the educational disparities these students face.

The combination of socioeconomic disadvantage and disability requires targeted interventions that address both sets of needs simultaneously. Chapter 4 explores specific examples.

Teacher expectations and bias

Teacher expectations play a crucial role in shaping student outcomes. These expectations include both the beliefs educators hold about a student's capabilities and the behaviours they exhibit in response to those beliefs. For disadvantaged students, expectations can significantly influence academic engagement, self-efficacy and achievement. Bias, whether conscious or not, exacerbates disparities and reinforces a cycle of underachievement.

The Pygmalion effect, or self-fulfilling prophecy, describes how students tend to perform in line with the expectations placed upon them. Teachers who anticipate high performance typically provide more encouragement, constructive feedback and challenging opportunities, which in turn foster achievement. Conversely, low expectations often result in less rigorous instruction, reduced attention and limited academic opportunities. Research consistently shows that disadvantaged students and neurodivergent students are at increased risk of being subjected to lower expectations due to societal stereotypes and systemic inequities (Rubie-Davies & Hattie, 2025).

Unconscious bias refers to the automatic attitudes or stereotypes that influence behaviour without conscious awareness. Educators may unintentionally interpret student behaviour through the lens of societal stereotypes – for example, viewing students from low-income backgrounds as less academically capable or mistaking attention difficulties for disinterest or laziness. A teacher might see a disadvantaged student arriving late or unprepared and assume laziness, when in reality the student is managing challenging circumstances at home.

These biases shape classroom interactions, grading practices and opportunities for participation, often reinforcing existing inequities (Good, 2010).

Students are often sensitive to these perceptions. When exposed consistently to low expectations, they may internalise these views, resulting in decreased motivation and self-belief.

Teacher expectations and bias are therefore pivotal in shaping learning trajectories. Low expectations restrict opportunities, reduce engagement and perpetuate disadvantage. In contrast, high expectations – when paired with appropriate support – can foster academic success and build lasting confidence.

Research consistently shows that teacher beliefs about student potential often become self-fulfilling prophecies (Rosenthal & Jacobson, 1968). While most teachers work hard to support all students, unconscious assumptions about ability can unintentionally restrict opportunities for those from marginalised backgrounds. Jussim & Harber (2005) found that teacher expectations had a particularly strong impact on vulnerable student groups. When teachers believe certain students have less potential, they may:

- set less challenging tasks
- reduce opportunities for metacognitive dialogue
- give less detailed feedback
- call on those students less often
- show less warmth in interactions.

These subtle differences accumulate over time, forming what Tenenbaum and Ruck (2007) termed 'differential treatment patterns' – a dynamic that entrenches educational inequality.

Addressing bias requires intentional professional development, reflective practice and inclusive instructional strategies. Chapter 3 explores how teachers can develop their own metacognitive awareness to recognise and counteract bias, maintain high expectations for all students, and create classroom environments that promote equity and achievement.

Given these multiple, interconnected barriers, what does research tell us about effective interventions? The Nuffield Foundation's 2025 report, *Educational Outcomes Across England*, examines the persistent attainment gaps between disadvantaged pupils and their peers. While increased funding, curriculum reforms and targeted tutoring are important, these measures alone are not enough to close educational gaps.

The report highlights that metacognitive strategies – explicitly teaching pupils to plan, monitor and evaluate their own learning – provide a powerful way to narrow attainment gaps. Research indicates that pupils who receive direct instruction in these strategies develop stronger memory, better problem-solving skills and greater resilience and self-regulation. These gains are especially valuable for pupils who do not have consistent learning support beyond the classroom.

Taken together, the evidence points to a clear direction: embedding metacognitive approaches within everyday teaching and wider policy offers one of the most effective means of reducing educational inequalities and supporting pupils to become more independent learners.

Metacognition as a pathway to independence

This book focuses on metacognition because traditional interventions – such as increased funding, smaller class sizes and curriculum reforms – while necessary, often address symptoms rather than root causes. Disadvantaged pupils, neurodivergent pupils and those with disabilities face a complex web of barriers, including socioeconomic, environmental, personal and psychological challenges. Limited academic support at home and low self-efficacy compound these difficulties, contributing to persistent attainment gaps across England. Metacognitive teaching offers a powerful complement: it equips pupils with transferable strategies for learning, thinking and self-regulation that apply across contexts and endure beyond the classroom. For disadvantaged pupils in particular, these strategies act as portable scaffolding, helping them learn not just what to think, but how to think – how to plan, monitor, evaluate and adapt their approach to tasks. This ability to regulate their own learning improves problem-solving, builds confidence and fosters resilience.

Understanding how metacognition works – and why it matters – is central to this book's approach. The 2025 Nuffield Foundation report, alongside evidence from the IFS and Institute for Government, highlights the critical importance of integrating cognitive skills development with structural and emotional support to maximise educational outcomes for disadvantaged pupils. Chapter 2 explores the theoretical foundations of metacognition in depth, unpacking how students develop awareness of their own thinking and learn to regulate their cognitive processes. The chapters that follow then demonstrate how metacognition can be taught, modelled and embedded across subjects and school, offering practical tools to help disadvantaged pupils become confident, independent learners. Throughout, this book maintains a clear focus on equity to show how metacognitive teaching can help close the advantage gap and ensure every pupil develops the thinking skills they need to thrive.

2 What is metacognition – and how does it support disadvantaged learners?

In Chapter 1, we explored the complex barriers that disadvantaged students face, from limited home support to systemic inequities. While these challenges are significant, research points to a powerful tool that can help level the playing field: metacognition. This chapter introduces the theory behind metacognition and explains why it's particularly effective for pupils facing disadvantage.

Education is about more than acquiring knowledge. It is about developing the ability to think critically, regulate one's learning and adapt to new challenges. Metacognition offers a structured approach to developing these abilities, and has gained increasing prominence in educational contexts for its potential to enhance pupils' learning outcomes.

Metacognitive theory is especially relevant for disadvantaged and neurodivergent students, who often face structural or personal barriers that impede independent learning. These learners may have gaps in prior knowledge due to limited resources or inconsistent support, making abstract concepts more difficult to grasp without careful scaffolding. Metacognition helps bridge these gaps by encouraging students to reflect on how they learn and adapt strategies to suit their needs.

Key term

Metacognition is 'thinking about thinking' (Flavell, 1979) – the ability to understand and reflect on one's own learning processes.

Understanding 'thinking about thinking'

Before exploring the theoretical framework of metacognition, it helps to understand what 'thinking about thinking' actually means in the context of everyday learning. The phrase can sound abstract, but the process is something we all experience.

When we engage in any learning task, two things happen simultaneously. First, there's the actual *doing* of the task – reading words, solving calculations, writing sentences. This is cognition: the mental work of processing information and completing activities. But alongside this, there's often a quieter process running in the background: an observing, monitoring, decision-making part of our mind that notices how the learning is going. This is metacognition: thinking about the thinking we're doing.

Consider a Year 6 pupil reading a passage about photosynthesis. As they read, one part of their mind processes the words, builds meaning from sentences and tries to construct understanding (cognition). But another part might simultaneously be noticing: *'I'm not sure I understand this bit about chlorophyll'*, *'This connects to what we learned last week about plants'* or *'I should probably reread that paragraph'*. This observing, monitoring, decision-making voice is metacognition at work.

The distinction matters profoundly because many pupils – particularly those from disadvantaged backgrounds – haven't developed this internal monitoring system. They may read without noticing when understanding breaks down, or attempt tasks without pausing to consider whether their approach is working. This isn't about ability; it's about exposure and explicit teaching.

What metacognition looks like in practice

Metacognition reveals itself through the questions learners ask themselves during tasks:

- *'What is this asking me to do?'* (understanding the task)
- *'Do I know anything about this already?'* (connecting to prior knowledge)
- *'Is this working? Am I making progress?'* (monitoring effectiveness)
- *'I'm confused – what could I try differently?'* (recognising difficulty and adapting)
- *'Did I answer the question I was actually asked?'* (evaluating outcomes).

For a pupil struggling with a challenging maths problem, metacognition is the process of recognising confusion, pausing to reconsider the approach and deciding to try a different strategy rather than simply giving up or continuing ineffectively. It's the capacity to step back from the task, observe one's own thinking and make strategic decisions about what to do next.

Why this matters for disadvantaged learners

Many pupils develop these internal monitoring processes naturally through rich interactions at home: parents who ask *'What do you think you should do first?'*, *'How will you know if you've got it right?'* or *'What made that tricky for you?'*. These conversations, repeated over years, gradually build the architecture of metacognitive thinking.

Disadvantaged pupils may not have had consistent access to such conversations. A child who has moved between multiple schools due to housing instability may never have been explicitly taught to pause and monitor their understanding. A pupil whose parents work multiple jobs and have limited time for homework support may not have experienced the reflective dialogue that builds metacognitive awareness. A young person experiencing trauma or instability at home may find that their cognitive resources are dedicated to managing emotional stress rather than monitoring their learning.

This doesn't mean these pupils lack potential. It means they need explicit, systematic teaching of the processes that others may have absorbed informally. When we teach metacognition, we're making the internal processes that support effective learning visible and accessible – processes that are often invisible to those who have developed them naturally.

Metacognitive moment: Making thinking visible

One of the most effective ways to understand metacognition is to see it in action. Consider how Ms Patel, a Year 5 teacher, makes her thinking visible when approaching a challenging word problem with her class:

'I'm reading this problem, and I notice there's a lot of information here. I'm feeling a bit overwhelmed, so I'm going to break it down. Let me underline the key information first... Now I need to decide which operation to use. The problem mentions 'how many more', so that tells me I'll need to compare two amounts using subtraction. But first, I need to calculate each amount separately. Let me check, am I understanding what the question is actually asking? Yes, I think so. Right, let me start with the first calculation...'

In this example, Ms Patel is doing more than solving a maths problem. She's making visible several metacognitive processes:

- noticing her own cognitive state ('I'm feeling overwhelmed')
- selecting a strategy to manage that state ('I'm going to break it down')
- monitoring her understanding ('Do I understand what the question is asking?')
- making strategic decisions based on her analysis ('I need to calculate each amount separately').

This demystifies the learning process for pupils watching. They see that successful learners don't simply 'know the answer' – they engage in strategic thinking, manage their own confusion and make deliberate choices about how to proceed. This visibility transforms learning from something magical that happens for some people into something systematic that can be learned.

Understanding metacognitive theory

Understanding the theoretical underpinnings of metacognition empowers teachers to implement metacognitive strategies more effectively in their classrooms. While it may be tempting to proceed directly to practical applications, exploring the research base and theoretical framework provides essential insights into why certain approaches prove effective, how metacognitive abilities develop, and what should be prioritised when teaching those skills to disadvantaged pupils. Metacognition is typically understood as comprising two key components:

- **metacognitive knowledge** – what pupils know about learning
- **metacognitive regulation** – how pupils manage their learning.

These components are explored in more depth in Chapters 4 and 5, but this chapter introduces them as a foundation.

Metacognitive knowledge

Metacognitive knowledge refers to what learners understand about how learning works, both in general and for themselves personally. This knowledge develops gradually and can be explicitly taught. For disadvantaged students, who often have had fewer opportunities to reflect on these learning processes, building this knowledge is particularly crucial.

It includes:

- **declarative knowledge** – knowing that different learning strategies exist
- **procedural knowledge** – knowing how to use those strategies effectively
- **conditional knowledge** – knowing when and why to use a particular strategy.

Each type plays a role in helping students become more strategic and independent learners. For example, a Year 4 pupil might know that summarising helps with comprehension (declarative), understand how to identify key points and rephrase them (procedural) and recognise that summarising is most useful for dense texts (conditional).

For students who have experienced inconsistent schooling or lack exposure to diverse learning contexts, developing conditional knowledge requires significant teacher support and multiple opportunities to practise in varied contexts. Chapter 4 explores these types of knowledge in more detail, with examples of how they develop and how teachers can support them.

Metacognitive regulation

Metacognitive regulation refers to the moment-by-moment decisions learners make during tasks. It includes five key processes:

- **planning** – setting goals and selecting strategies
- **connecting** – linking new content to prior knowledge
- **checking** – establishing and understanding what the task is asking
- **monitoring** – tracking progress and noticing confusion
- **evaluating** – assessing effectiveness and planning next steps.

Each process can be explicitly taught and modelled in the classroom. For example, in a writing lesson a student might plan by brainstorming arguments, connect by recalling prior knowledge, monitor by checking sentence clarity, and evaluate by reviewing their draft against success criteria. Chapter 5 explores how to teach each of these processes through the PCCME cycle — a structured approach built around Plan, Connect, Check, Monitor and Evaluate.

How metacognitive abilities develop

Metacognitive abilities develop gradually from early childhood onwards, with explicit teaching accelerating this development at any age (Brown, 1987; Flavell, 1979). While the pace varies among learners, the progression is consistent: children move from basic awareness of their thinking to increasingly sophisticated self-regulation strategies. Understanding this developmental trajectory is crucial when planning age-appropriate metacognitive instruction. Chapter 4 explores the stages of metacognitive development in detail, with practical guidance for supporting pupils at each stage.

The impact of metacognition

Research summary: Metacognitive skills and achievement

- Study: Wang et al. (1990) – meta-analysis across multiple studies, age groups and subjects.
- Key finding: Metacognitive skills were found to be a stronger predictor of academic success than IQ, explaining approximately 40 per cent of the variance in pupil achievement.
- Practical implication: Teaching metacognitive strategies can be especially powerful for pupils who lack confidence or face academic challenges. Developing these 'thinking skills' helps learners overcome barriers and creates a more level playing field.

Metacognition plays a critical role in problem-solving and reasoning. In mathematics, success depends not only on subject-specific knowledge but also on pupils' ability to monitor their thinking and manage learning resources efficiently (Schoenfeld, 1985). In reading, deep comprehension relies on metacognitive strategies such as predicting, summarising and clarifying information (Pressley & Afflerbach, 1995). Across subjects, self-regulated learners (those who can plan, monitor and reflect on their learning) consistently demonstrate higher academic achievement and resilience (Zimmerman, 2002).

Why this matters for disadvantaged students

The Education Endowment Foundation (2018) identifies metacognition and self-regulation approaches as among the most cost-effective ways to raise attainment, particularly for disadvantaged pupils. When students learn to ask themselves questions like *'What is this task asking of me?'* or *'What could I do differently next time?'*, they begin to take a more active role in their learning. This shift is especially powerful for those who may have internalised failure or developed fixed mindsets due to repeated academic setbacks.

Metacognitive instruction helps redirect focus from perceived ability to strategy use and effort, reinforcing the idea that learning is a process that can be improved. It also supports emotional resilience, as students learn to reflect, adapt and persist through difficulty. Metacognition also supports emotional regulation and resilience. When students learn to pause, evaluate their approach and adjust accordingly, they reduce the fear of failure and develop a growth mindset (Dweck, 2006). This mindset is especially critical for disadvantaged learners, who may have internalised narratives of academic inadequacy.

By developing the ability to plan, monitor and evaluate their thinking, teachers equip pupils with tools to take control of their learning – even in the face of external barriers. This self-awareness fosters resilience, confidence and independence: qualities that are especially crucial for learners who lack consistent academic support or face social and emotional difficulties.

Consider a pupil who has moved frequently due to housing instability. Having attended four different schools and missed significant chunks of learning, they may not have had consistent exposure to classroom routines and learning strategies. As a result, they often feel lost and uncertain about how to approach new tasks. Without explicit support, they may struggle to plan their work, monitor their progress or evaluate what's working – not because they lack ability, but because they haven't yet been taught how to think about their thinking.

Similarly, some pupils come from households where parents work multiple jobs and have limited time for homework support. These learners may not have experienced reflective conversations about learning. When faced with a challenging maths problem, they are more likely to give up than to think strategically. For pupils with additional learning needs – such as dyscalculia – the absence of metacognitive tools can compound existing challenges.

In such cases, metacognitive instruction can be transformative. By explicitly teaching strategies such as planning, monitoring and evaluating, teachers help learners take greater ownership of their thinking. These approaches are explored in detail in Chapters 4 and 5, including how to model them effectively and embed them through the PCCME cycle.

Metacognitive strategies also help students persist through difficulty, reducing feelings of frustration and helplessness (Duckworth & Gross, 2014). A study by Dignath and Büttner (2008) found that pupils who received metacognitive instruction not only improved their academic performance but also demonstrated higher motivation and self-regulation skills compared to peers who did not receive such instruction.

Over time, metacognitive instruction builds confidence, persistence and adaptability across subjects and contexts. For disadvantaged students, it offers a way to navigate learning more deliberately, bridging gaps in prior experience and fostering long-term resilience. In this way, metacognitive teaching does more than improve academic outcomes; it empowers disadvantaged pupils with lifelong strategies for navigating learning and overcoming challenges with greater confidence.

How metacognitive instruction transforms learning

Explicitly teaching metacognitive strategies gives pupils ownership over their learning. It demystifies the learning process and equips them with a reliable structure they can draw on, even when external support is limited. For pupils from disadvantaged backgrounds, this shift from passive to active learning can be transformational.

The structured, explicit nature of metacognitive instruction is especially effective for pupils with additional learning needs. Consistent routines and clear frameworks help reduce cognitive load and build confidence. When pupils learn *how* to learn alongside *what* to learn, they develop transferable skills that support progress across all subjects and beyond the classroom.

From theory to practice

To be effective, metacognitive strategies must be taught deliberately and reinforced consistently. Many pupils, particularly those from disadvantaged backgrounds, may not have encountered structured approaches to thinking about their learning. Without explicit instruction, they are unlikely to develop these skills independently.

The strategies that follow are carefully designed applications of metacognitive theory, each targeting specific aspects of metacognitive development. When implemented in the classroom, they do more than teach techniques; they help build the cognitive architecture that underpins independent learning.

Implementation checkpoint: Check your understanding of metacognition

Before moving to Chapter 3 on teacher metacognition, assess your understanding and readiness:

- ✓ Could I explain the difference between cognition and metacognition to a colleague?
- ✓ Can I explain the difference between metacognitive knowledge and regulation?
- ✓ Do I understand why disadvantaged students particularly benefit from explicit metacognitive instruction?
- ✓ What barriers might my students face in developing these skills?

If you cannot confidently answer most questions, consider rereading relevant sections or discussing with colleagues before proceeding.

Key takeaways

- Metacognition means 'thinking about thinking' – the capacity to observe, monitor and direct one's own learning processes while engaged in tasks.
- Cognition is doing the task; metacognition is the internal voice that asks *'Do I understand this?'*, *'Is this working?'* and *'What should I try next?'*.
- Many pupils develop metacognitive awareness through rich home conversations; disadvantaged pupils often need explicit, systematic teaching of these processes.
- Metacognition comprises two components: metacognitive knowledge (what pupils understand about learning) and metacognitive regulation (how they manage their learning moment-by-moment).
- Research shows metacognitive instruction is one of the most effective strategies for raising attainment, particularly for disadvantaged pupils.

3 Teachers' metacognition

Teaching is an inherently metacognitive profession. Effective educators continually reflect on their own thinking: how they plan, execute and adapt lessons to meet the varied needs of their students. At its heart, teaching involves continuous reflection, problem-solving and adaptation. From anticipating pupil needs to responding to confusion mid-task, teachers engage in the same strategic thinking they aim to cultivate in their pupils: planning, connecting, monitoring and evaluating. These metacognitive processes are not abstract ideas – they play out in the everyday realities of classroom practice.

This chapter explores how teachers can develop and harness their metacognitive capacities to foster more equitable learning environments. We will examine why teacher metacognition matters especially for disadvantaged students, how to plan and adapt instruction metacognitively, how to model thinking for pupils, and how to use reflection and school culture to strengthen practice.

The role of metacognition in teaching

Metacognition in teaching involves both metacognitive knowledge (understanding one's own cognitive processes and teaching strategies) and metacognitive regulation (actively managing and adapting instructional decisions). Teachers who engage in metacognitive practice are better equipped to meet the diverse needs of their pupils, particularly those from disadvantaged backgrounds who may require additional support (EEF, 2018; Schön, 1983).

For disadvantaged pupils, teacher metacognition can be the difference between learning that feels accessible and learning that feels out of reach. When teachers actively reflect on their practice – questioning assumptions, monitoring student responses and adjusting their approaches – they create more inclusive and responsive learning environments.

Metacognition and disadvantage

Disadvantaged pupils often face compounding barriers: limited access to resources, inconsistent home support and fewer opportunities to develop independent learning strategies. Research consistently shows that these students benefit most from explicit instruction and structured support (Gorard & See, 2013).

As explored in Chapter 1, students' familiarity with academic discourse varies widely, shaped by early language experiences and broader structural factors. When teachers understand this, it transforms how they interpret student responses and plan instruction. A pupil who appears 'unmotivated' may simply lack the planning strategies more advantaged peers absorbed at home. Another who 'won't try' might be protecting themselves from repeated failure.

In such contexts, teaching demands more than subject knowledge; it requires moment-by-moment responsiveness. Teachers should attend to subtle signals, think critically in the moment and adapt their methods with clear purpose. Metacognitive habits – anticipating difficulties, monitoring impact, evaluating decisions – enable this kind of adaptive teaching, helping educators meet diverse needs without lowering expectations.

Every teaching day involves complex metacognitive processes. Before lessons begin, teachers plan by considering learning objectives, anticipating difficulties, selecting strategies and preparing materials. During instruction, they monitor student engagement and understanding, connect new content to prior learning and adjust in real time. Afterwards, they evaluate what worked, what didn't and how to improve future instruction.

For teachers working with disadvantaged students, metacognitive awareness is especially critical (EEF, 2018). These pupils often arrive at school with fewer opportunities to develop self-regulation skills, limited exposure to academic discourse, and additional emotional and social challenges that can hinder learning (Jensen, 2009). Again, teachers must be attuned to subtle cues, able to adapt instruction in the moment, and ready to provide the explicit scaffolding these learners need.

In contexts where students arrive with strong academic foundations, teaching often allows for established routines and assumptions about prior knowledge. In contrast, where students face significant barriers, teachers must constantly monitor understanding, adapt communication, offer emotional support and differentiate instruction – while still maintaining high expectations alongside engaging and culturally relevant content. Teachers who regularly evaluate the impact of their teaching are better equipped to identify and address barriers to learning. This might involve scaffolding tasks, differentiating instruction or modifying feedback: all of which require deep awareness of both the learner and the learning environment.

This heightened demand for responsive teaching makes metacognitive awareness essential. Teachers who reflect on their thinking, question assumptions and adapt their approaches are better equipped to meet their students' needs.

Anticipating student needs through metacognitive planning

Effective lesson planning for disadvantaged students requires sophisticated metacognitive processes that go beyond selecting activities and materials. Teachers must think strategically about how to structure learning experiences that build academic and emotional competence, while anticipating potential barriers to engagement.

This kind of planning involves more than choosing what to teach – it means anticipating how students will experience the learning and what supports they might need to access it fully. Metacognitive teachers consider not only what students need to learn, but also how their backgrounds, experiences and emotional states might affect their ability to engage.

This planning process involves asking questions like:

- *'What prior knowledge are my pupils likely to have, and what gaps might exist?'*
- *'How can I connect this content to their lived experiences?'*
- *'What emotional or social factors might interfere with learning today?'*
- *'Which pupils will need additional scaffolding, and how can I provide it without making them feel different?'*

Teaching pupils to plan their learning transforms them from passive recipients of information into active strategists. However, many disadvantaged pupils may not yet have developed the executive function skills needed for effective planning. Teachers can guide them through this process by providing structured templates and modelling the planning process aloud.

For pupils who have experienced inconsistent schooling, open-ended tasks can feel overwhelming. By offering clear frameworks and modelling strategic thinking, teachers equip students with the tools they need to approach learning with confidence.

A metacognitive teacher recognises that a student who gives one-word answers may not lack understanding – they may simply be unfamiliar with the elaborate explanations valued in school settings.

Executing lessons with metacognitive responsiveness

Metacognitive awareness transforms how teachers interpret student responses. Instead of seeing brief responses as evidence of limited thinking, metacognitive teachers ask: *'How can I scaffold this student to share their understanding in ways that feel accessible to them?'*, *'What cultural strengths are they bringing that I might not be recognising?'*, *'How can I model the kinds of academic discourse that will serve them in school while validating their existing communication patterns?'*.

Self-regulated teachers demonstrate greater instructional clarity, emotional resilience and responsiveness to student needs. They pause and recalibrate when a lesson is not going as planned, rather than rigidly adhering to a pre-set script. This involves moment-by-moment decision-making based on careful observation of student responses, emotional states and engagement levels.

Teacher metacognitive regulation involves the active management of instruction based on ongoing assessment of student needs and lesson effectiveness. This might include switching teaching strategies mid-lesson when students appear confused, providing additional emotional support when a student seems distressed, or adjusting the pace of instruction based on student responses.

Metacognitive moment: Adapting in real time

During a Year 4 maths lesson on fractions, Mr Williams noticed several pupils looking confused when he explained equivalent fractions using the traditional method. Rather than continuing with his planned approach, he paused and reflected aloud: 'I can see this isn't clicking yet. Let me try showing this a different way.'

He switched to a visual approach using fraction walls and real objects, explicitly narrating his decision: 'I'm noticing that the numbers aren't making sense to you, so I'm going to use something you can see and touch instead. Sometimes when one way doesn't work, we need to try another strategy.'

This metacognitive transparency achieved two things: it modelled adaptive thinking for pupils, and it removed any sense that their confusion was a failure. The message was clear – skilled learners adjust their approach when needed.

For disadvantaged students, this regulation often needs to be more frequent and more nuanced. Teachers must monitor not just academic understanding but also emotional states, engagement levels and social dynamics. They must be prepared to pause instruction to address emotional needs, reteach concepts in multiple ways and provide additional scaffolding that other students might not require.

Effective teachers constantly monitor multiple data streams during instruction, including student facial expressions and body language, the quality of student responses and questions, levels of engagement and participation, the emotional climate in the classroom, and the pacing and timing of activities. For disadvantaged students, metacognitive regulation must be especially sensitive to emotional and social cues. A student who becomes withdrawn may be experiencing stress, confusion or overwhelm. Teachers who monitor these subtle shifts can respond before small issues become larger barriers.

Teacher self-regulation supports professional wellbeing. The ability to manage stress, set realistic expectations and maintain perspective helps teachers remain effective over time. In high-pressure environments, teachers who are emotionally self-regulated are better positioned to model calmness, perseverance and problem-solving for their students.

Adaptable teachers like those described here are better equipped to support learning, especially for students with varied backgrounds, learning styles or additional needs (Corno, 2008). Adaptability is particularly important in classrooms with high levels of disadvantage, where students often bring external barriers to learning, such as socio-emotional challenges, language gaps or inconsistent prior knowledge.

Questioning cultural assumptions

Metacognitive teaching is not just about helping pupils regulate their learning – it's also about teachers reflecting on their own assumptions. Effective metacognitive educators question what they consider 'good' participation, recognising that such expectations may be culturally specific. Research by Gay (2010) on culturally responsive teaching highlights the importance of critical self-reflection, especially when working with diverse populations. Reflect on the following example. What may appear as a lack of engagement or poor metacognitive skills can often reflect cultural mismatches rather than student deficits.

Mr Ahmed, a secondary English teacher in East London, noticed that several pupils from Somali backgrounds rarely volunteered answers, despite clearly engaging with the texts. Rather than interpreting this as passivity or misunderstanding, he reflected on his own assumptions about classroom participation. He realised he had been expecting immediate, confident verbal responses – a communication style valued in some cultures but not universal. Cross-cultural research notes that many Somali diasporic families draw on communication traditions that emphasise reflection, attentive listening and well-formed contributions over quick turn-taking, as well as a preference for speaking at the appropriate moment in group settings. None of these tendencies are fixed or universal, but they illustrate how participation norms can vary widely across communities. Once Mr Ahmed recognised this, he adapted his approach to include written responses, paired discussions and thinking time before whole-class sharing. Participation increased dramatically. The pupils weren't disengaged – they simply needed participation structures that aligned with their communication preferences. The mismatch wasn't between the pupils' culture and school, but between Mr Ahmed's assumptions about what "active participation" looks like and a set of communication norms common in many collectivist, multilingual or diasporic families, including some Somali ones.

This example illustrates how metacognitive teaching, when paired with cultural responsiveness, can foster equity and inclusion. It empowers pupils to engage in ways that feel authentic to them, while encouraging teachers to reflect on how their practices support or hinder that engagement.

Teachers as metacognitive models

One of the most powerful ways teachers use their metacognition is by making their thinking visible to pupils. When teachers think aloud – narrating their thought processes, acknowledging confusion, demonstrating how they work through problems – they model the internal dialogue that skilled learners use.

For disadvantaged pupils, who may never have heard an adult articulate their thinking process, this modelling is invaluable. It demystifies learning and shows that capable thinkers don't have all the answers immediately – they use strategies to work things out.

However, effective modelling is a skill that requires practice and understanding. Chapter 4 explores in detail how to model metacognitive thinking effectively across different subjects and age groups. For now, the key point is that teachers must first develop their own metacognitive awareness before they can model it for pupils. You cannot make your thinking visible if you're not consciously aware of it yourself.

Classroom snapshot: Reflective practice in action

Ms Okafor, a Year 3 teacher in Birmingham, regularly models her metacognitive thinking during guided reading. When encountering a difficult word, she doesn't simply provide the definition – she narrates her thinking strategy:

'I don't know this word "camouflage". Let me think about what I could do. I could sound it out... cam-ou-flage. That doesn't help me understand what it means. I could look at the picture – I see an animal that's hard to see against the tree. I could read the sentence again and see if the context gives me clues: "The lizard's camouflage helped it hide from predators." Ah! It must mean something that helps you hide or blend in.'

By modelling this process explicitly, Ms Okafor showed her pupils – many of whom were EAL learners – that not knowing a word is normal, and that there are multiple strategies for working out meaning. Over time, pupils began using these same strategies independently.

Professional reflection as a metacognitive tool

Reflection is the cornerstone of metacognitive teaching practice. It enables teachers to examine their instructional decisions, evaluate their effectiveness and identify areas for growth. Structured reflection moves beyond surface-level observations ('the lesson went well') to deeper analysis of why certain strategies work and how practices might improve.

For teachers working with disadvantaged pupils, reflection serves several critical functions: it helps identify unconscious biases or assumptions that might be limiting pupil potential, it reveals patterns in which pupils struggle and why, it surfaces successful strategies worth replicating, and it builds the habit of questioning and adapting rather than relying on autopilot teaching.

Effective reflection asks probing questions:

- *'What did I assume pupils already knew? Were those assumptions accurate?'*
- *'Which pupils thrived today? Which struggled? What patterns do I notice?'*
- *'What did I do when I noticed confusion? How effective was my response?'*
- *'Did I maintain high expectations whilst providing appropriate support?'*
- *'What would I do differently next time, and why?'*

These questions promote deeper insights that can lead to meaningful change. By interrogating their own practices, teachers become more aware of biases, assumptions and areas for growth, leading to more inclusive teaching strategies that particularly benefit disadvantaged students.

Reflection also fosters teacher autonomy. Rather than relying solely on external evaluation or fixed curricula, reflective teachers develop the internal resources to assess and enhance their own practice. As Brookfield argued, the critically reflective teacher is better able to 'uncover and challenge assumptions' that may otherwise go unexamined (1995, p. 743).

When teachers share their reflections in communities of practice – such as coaching partnerships or staff meetings – they not only refine their own thinking but contribute to a culture of collective improvement, promoting deeper learning across teams and schools.

Quick guide

Teachers can build reflection into their practice through various methods. Brief post-lesson jottings capture immediate insights before they're forgotten while weekly reflection prompts encourage deeper analysis of patterns. Peer observation and discussion can provide external perspectives on practice, and video-recording lessons for self-review can reveal dynamics teachers might miss in the moment.

Reflection prompts

After a lesson:

- What surprised me about pupils' responses today?
- Which pupil did I struggle to reach? Why might that be?
- When did I adjust my plan? What prompted that decision? How effective was it?

Weekly:

- Which pupils haven't I had individual conversations with this week?
- What patterns do I notice in who participates and how?
- What assumptions did I make that turned out to be incorrect?

Termly:

- How have my most disadvantaged pupils progressed?
- What strategies have been most effective with pupils who face barriers to learning?
- What do I need to learn or develop to better serve my pupils?

Developing teacher metacognition

Developing metacognitive capacity requires deliberate practice, supportive structures and ongoing professional learning. Individual teachers can strengthen their metacognitive awareness, but schools can accelerate this development through collaborative approaches.

Professional learning communities that focus specifically on metacognitive teaching provide space for teachers to share reflections, analyse pupils' work together and problem-solve around common challenges. When teachers examine videos of their practice or discuss specific instructional moments, they develop stronger metacognitive awareness.

Instructional coaching that uses a metacognitive approach – helping teachers notice their own thinking patterns, question assumptions and try new strategies – builds capacity more effectively than directive feedback. Coaches who ask *'What did you notice?'* and *'What were you thinking when you made that decision?'* help teachers develop the reflective habits central to metacognitive practice.

School leaders can also create conditions that support teacher metacognition. This can be achieved by: protecting time for reflection and collaborative planning, modelling metacognitive thinking in their own leadership practice, celebrating adaptive teaching rather than perfect lesson execution, and providing access to professional learning focused on responsive, equity-oriented instruction.

Implementation checkpoint: Building metacognitive habits

Reflection doesn't require hours of additional time. Try these quick strategies:

✓ After each lesson, jot down one thing that surprised you about pupils' responses.

✓ Once a week, ask yourself: *'Which pupil did I struggle to reach this week? Why might that be?'*

✓ Monthly, review your seating plan and identify pupils you haven't spoken to individually – seek them out next week.

✓ Each term, record yourself teaching for 10 minutes and note your questioning patterns: Who are you calling on? How long do you wait for answers?

✓ Keep a 'curious moments' log – note instances when pupils' responses challenged your assumptions.

Start with one strategy for a month before adding another.

Key takeaways

- Teacher metacognition – thinking about your own thinking as you teach – is essential for equitable practice.
- Metacognitive teachers plan by anticipating barriers, execute lessons responsively and reflect systematically.
- For disadvantaged pupils, teachers' metacognitive capacity can compensate for limited home support and cultural capital.
- Effective metacognitive teaching requires noticing subtle cues, questioning assumptions and adapting in real time.
- Developing teacher metacognition requires deliberate practice, peer collaboration and supportive school structures.
- Before you can teach metacognition to pupils, you must develop it in yourself.

Reflection prompts

For educators:

- How consciously aware am I of my thinking during lessons?
- When did I last adjust a plan mid-lesson based on what I noticed about pupils?
- Which of my assumptions about pupils might be limiting their potential?
- How do I respond when pupils don't understand my initial explanation?

For school leaders:

- How does our school culture support or hinder teacher reflection?
- Do teachers feel safe to admit confusion or adjust plans without being judged?
- What structures exist for collaborative reflection on practice?
- How do we model metacognitive thinking in our leadership?

Next steps

1 Choose one reflective practice strategy from the Implementation Checkpoint and commit to it for a month.

2 Observe a colleague's lesson with a specific focus on their metacognitive responsiveness.

3 Audio-record one of your lessons and analyse your questioning patterns – who participates? How do you respond to confusion?

4 Start a brief teaching journal to capture metacognitive insights – just 2–3 minutes after each day.

5 Find an accountability partner and share one metacognitive reflection weekly.

6 Read Chapter 4 to learn how to model metacognitive thinking effectively for your pupils.

4 Metacognitive modelling

In Chapter 3, we explored how teachers develop their own metacognitive capacity – the foundation for effective teaching. This chapter focuses on the next critical step: making that thinking visible to pupils through metacognitive modelling.

Metacognitive modelling helps pupils internalise the thinking strategies needed for independent learning – particularly those who may struggle with self-regulation and confidence. By verbalising their thought processes in real time, teachers make their thinking visible, offering students a clear framework for planning, monitoring and reflecting. Over time, repeated exposure to this modelling enables students to adopt these habits of mind and apply them independently.

As children move from early years to secondary school, they gradually take on more responsibility for their thinking. Metacognitive modelling – talking through how we think – supports this development by showing students how to manage their learning more effectively. Muncaster and Clarke (2017) found that guiding pupils step-by-step through planning, reflection and adjustment leads to deeper learning – especially for disadvantaged students who may not have had consistent exposure to these strategies at home.

This chapter explores what makes metacognitive modelling effective, how to adapt it for different ages and needs, and how to avoid common pitfalls.

Understanding metacognitive modelling

Key term

Metacognitive modelling is the explicit demonstration of thinking processes by teachers to make invisible mental strategies visible and accessible to students. It bridges the gap between teacher knowledge and student practice.

Metacognitive modelling goes beyond simply showing pupils what to do – it reveals how to think. When teachers explain their mental processes aloud, students gain insight into the decision-making, problem-solving and self-regulation strategies that underpin effective learning.

This process engages both metacognitive awareness (knowing what strategies to use) and metacognitive regulation (knowing when and how to apply them). Flavell's (1979) foundational work on metacognition established that learners benefit significantly from observing expert thinking, particularly when teachers verbalise their monitoring and adjustment processes during tasks.

Dignath & Veenman (2020) confirmed that explicit modelling of metacognitive strategies is especially beneficial for struggling learners, including those from disadvantaged backgrounds. For students with limited exposure to rich language interactions or problem-solving discussions at home, classroom modelling becomes a vital source of cognitive scaffolding.

Why metacognitive modelling matters for disadvantaged students

As explored in Chapter 1, disadvantaged students face multiple barriers to learning, and research shows that teacher expectations can inadvertently compound these challenges through differential treatment patterns. However, metacognitive modelling serves as a powerful equity strategy that actively counters these effects.

Metacognitive modelling is particularly powerful for challenging low expectations because it:

- **makes thinking accessible.** Verbalising thought processes provides disadvantaged students with the kind of 'thinking aloud' that more advantaged peers may hear regularly at home.

- **sets high expectations.** Rather than lowering cognitive demand, modelling shows struggling students how to tackle complex tasks, reinforcing the belief that all students can succeed when given appropriate scaffolding.

- **builds agency.** When students learn to monitor and regulate their own thinking, they develop a sense of control over their learning which supports resilience and motivation.

- **provides a replicable model.** Unlike vague encouragement, metacognitive modelling offers concrete strategies students can observe, practice and internalise.

Mercer and Littleton (2007) found that students from disadvantaged backgrounds showed significant gains in reasoning and problem-solving when consistently exposed to explicit modelling of thinking strategies.

Meeting diverse needs through metacognitive modelling

For disadvantaged students, metacognitive modelling helps bridge gaps in prior knowledge and learning experiences. Consistent exposure to explicit thinking strategies enables pupils to internalise effective cognitive habits, building long-term academic resilience.

As Chapter 1 highlighted, these students face varied barriers that metacognitive modelling can help address:

- Students with EAL requirements benefit from visual and gestural demonstrations alongside verbal modelling. Use home language labels where possible and accept gestural or pictorial responses.
- Pupils from high-mobility backgrounds need explicit connection-making to rebuild learning continuity. Make links between current and previous learning explicit.
- Those with undiagnosed learning differences respond well to multimodal thinking strategies. Break complex processes into smaller steps and use visual supports.
- Students experiencing trauma or instability may need emotional regulation to be modelled alongside cognitive approaches. Create predictable routines and safe learning environments.
- Children from cultures emphasising collective learning may express metacognitive awareness through collaborative problem-solving and observation rather than individual articulation.

Crucially, metacognitive awareness may be expressed differently across cultures and individual needs. Through observation, collaborative problem-solving or respectful questioning, effective modelling recognises and responds to this diversity.

The impact on learning

Metacognitive modelling enhances learning by:

- promoting active engagement over the passive receipt of information
- developing self-regulation through guided practice

- building resilience and adaptability by showing that learning involves setbacks and adjustments
- providing disadvantaged students with tools for cognitive development.

Research summary: Metacognitive modelling and disadvantaged students

- The study: Mercer & Littleton (2007) carried out long-term classroom observations in schools serving pupils from a range of socioeconomic backgrounds.
- Key findings: Their research demonstrated that pupils achieved notable gains in reasoning and problem-solving when teachers consistently modelled their thinking aloud. This 'thinking together' approach – where educators verbalise their own decision-making and problem-solving strategies – was particularly effective for students who may not have had regular exposure to such language and learning habits at home.
- Practical implications: Structured and explicit metacognitive modelling helps to close gaps in access to academic discourse. For disadvantaged pupils it provides a vital scaffold for developing independent learning strategies, offering clear, repeatable examples of how to approach tasks, reflect on progress and adapt thinking. This kind of modelling not only supports cognitive development but also communicates high expectations and builds learner confidence.

Developmental progression of metacognitive modelling

Metacognitive development typically follows a progression from initial awareness to the full internalisation of thinking strategies. Understanding this journey is crucial when working with disadvantaged students, as it helps educators to identify where each learner is in their metacognitive growth and then tailor support accordingly.

It is important to note that metacognitive strategies remain fundamentally the same across all developmental stages; what changes is the depth of application, level of independence and complexity. While young learners require explicit modelling and support to transfer strategies between contexts, older students are expected to self-regulate and transfer independently – though some primary school pupils demonstrate this capability earlier than others.

Students with emotional and behavioural challenges often struggle with self-regulation and may resist metacognitive strategies. When introducing metacognitive modelling to these students:

- begin with short, highly structured modelling sessions (3–5 minutes) to build tolerance
- use visual supports alongside verbal modelling to help maintain focus
- explicitly model emotional regulation alongside cognitive strategies (*'I'm feeling stuck and frustrated, so I'm going to take a deep breath and try a different approach'*)
- provide immediate opportunities for success through scaffolded practice
- acknowledge and celebrate small improvements in strategy use.

The four-stage model presented here – moving from foundational awareness through strategic thinking and reflection to independent self-regulation – provides a practical roadmap for developing metacognitive skills in pupils who have had limited previous exposure to metacognitive thinking. It enables educators to scaffold learning in a structured, responsive way, helping all students build the habits of mind needed for confident, independent learning.

Stage 1: Establishing foundational awareness

Table 1: Stage 1 – foundational awareness

Key characteristics	Teacher's role	Signs of progress
Basic recognition that thinking is a process	Name thinking processes explicitly (*'You're making a prediction!'*)	Student begins to use thinking vocabulary
Beginning ability to articulate simple thought processes	Ask simple reflective questions about thinking	Student notices when they don't understand
Emerging awareness of different learning strategies	Provide concrete supports for metacognitive language	Student can explain simple strategies they use
Recognition of when understanding breaks down	Model noticing confusion and seeking clarity	Student asks for help when stuck

In early childhood education, metacognitive modelling begins with fostering children's basic awareness of how they think and learn (Table 1). While young children are naturally inquisitive, they need structured guidance to begin articulating their own thought processes and recognising how they learn best.

Metacognition develops gradually, moving from simple awareness to independent self-regulation (Table 2). In the early stages, learners start to notice their thinking and use simple strategies with adult support. As they progress, they become more able to monitor and adjust their thinking with prompts and scaffolds (Table 3). Eventually, they develop into self-regulated learners who can confidently apply metacognitive strategies across different contexts without external support.

Key strategies for developing foundational metacognitive awareness

1. Thinking aloud and teacher modelling

One of the most effective ways to develop metacognitive awareness in young children is through teacher modelling. When educators verbalise their thinking – such as predicting a story's outcome or reasoning through a maths task – students gain insight into how to approach learning in a structured way (Veenman et al., 2006). This is particularly beneficial for disadvantaged students as it provides explicit guidance on processing information and developing problem-solving strategies they may not encounter elsewhere.

Metacognitive moment: Across different contexts

Mathematics – Year 3 with diverse learners
In Mr Patel's classroom, students are exploring multiplication through hands-on activities. 'Let's see how many groups of three we can make with these counters…' For Nour, a recent refugee from Syria with limited English proficiency, Mr Patel models counting aloud while using visuals and gestures to reinforce concepts. For Tyler, who struggles with working memory difficulties, he provides a number line and breaks problems into smaller, manageable steps. Meanwhile, for Sofia, who thrives on peer collaboration but gets distracted easily, he pairs her with a supportive partner for guided practice.

PE – Year 4 gymnastics

During a gymnastics session, Ms Lopez models her movements out loud: 'I'm going to balance on one foot. I need to keep my arms steady and my core engaged.' For children with balance difficulties, she demonstrates each movement slowly and breaks routines into smaller steps. For those who feel anxious about performing, she praises effort and concentration rather than just the final pose. For more confident pupils, she encourages them to experiment with variations while reflecting on what worked well and what could be improved.

2. Simple reflection questions

At this foundational stage, reflection questions should be concrete and accessible:

- *'What did you notice?'*
- *'What helped you understand?'*
- *'How did you work that out?'*
- *'What was tricky about that?'*

These questions help children begin to articulate their thinking without overwhelming them with complex metacognitive language.

3. Using visual and concrete supports

Young children benefit significantly from visual representations of thinking. These can include using hats or characters to embody different types of thinking, or simple charts that separate *'what I know'* from *'what I wonder'*. Gestures can also represent various thinking strategies, and picture prompts are useful for encouraging reflection.

Table 2: Implementation sequence – building Stage 1 awareness

Weeks 1–2	Establish thinking vocabulary	• Introduce three key words with actions: 'predict' (hand to forehead), 'notice' (point to eyes), 'wonder' (finger to temple) • Point out when children naturally use these processes: *'I see you predicting!'*

Weeks 3–4	Add simple reflection	• *'I notice you're wondering – that's what good learners do'* • For reluctant speakers: Use thumbs up/down or emotion cards • For those with attention challenges: Limit to one reflection prompt per session
Weeks 5–6	Encourage peer recognition	• *'Can you spot when your partner is noticing something?'* • For children from cultures emphasising collective learning: Frame as 'helping our learning community'

Stage 2: Developing strategic thinking

Table 3: Stage 2 – strategic development

Key characteristics	Teacher's role	Signs of progress
Awareness of multiple strategies for learning	Model strategy selection process	Student tries different approaches when stuck
Beginning ability to select appropriate strategies	Provide strategy menus and choices	Student can explain why they chose a particular strategy
Can explain reasoning behind strategy choices	Encourage strategy comparison	Student begins to evaluate strategy effectiveness
Starts to monitor strategy effectiveness	Support students in explaining their thinking	Student starts to plan before beginning tasks

Stage 3: Building reflective practices

Table 4: Stage 3 – reflective practice

Key characteristics	Teacher's role	Signs of progress
Regular self-evaluation of learning	Structure regular reflection opportunities	Student regularly evaluates their learning
Ability to adjust strategies based on reflection	Model self-evaluation processes	Student adjusts approach based on reflection
Growing awareness of personal learning preferences	Encourage strategy adjustment	Student sets learning goals
Can articulate what makes learning effective	Support goal-setting based on reflection	Student identifies personal learning preferences

In upper primary years, students develop sophisticated reflective capabilities (Table 4). They learn to evaluate their learning systematically and make adjustments based on their reflections.

Key strategies for building reflective practices

1. Structured reflection routines

Metacognitive moment: Reflecting at the end of a lesson

Year 6 teacher Ms Hudson incorporates daily reflection into her lessons: *'Before we finish our science investigation, let's think about what went well, what we found challenging, and what we'd do differently next time. I'll model my thinking first, then you can share yours with a partner.'*

2. Learning journals and self-assessment

Students maintain learning journals where they record not just what they learned, but how they learned it. Prompts might include:

- *'The strategy that helped me most today was...'*
- *'I found it difficult when...'*
- *'Next time I would...'*

Stage 4: Achieving independent self-regulation

Table 5: Stage 4 – independent self-regulation

Key characteristics	Teacher's role	Signs of progress
Autonomous planning and goal-setting	Provide minimal scaffolding	Student independently plans learning approaches
Self-directed strategy selection and adjustment	Encourage student-led learning	Student self-monitors and adjusts without prompts

Key characteristics	Teacher's role	Signs of progress
Sophisticated self-monitoring	Support complex strategy integration	Student applies strategies flexibly across contexts
Independent evaluation and reflection	Foster metacognitive transfer across subjects	Student demonstrates academic resilience

At this advanced stage, typically seen in upper primary and secondary years, students demonstrate autonomous self-regulation (Table 5). They can plan, monitor and evaluate their learning with minimal external support.

Key strategies for supporting independent self-regulation

1. Gradual release of responsibility

Systematically reduce scaffolding while providing support through a clear progression:

- **initial scaffolding:** full teacher guidance with explicit modelling
- **collaborative practice:** shared responsibility with guided decision-making
- **guided practice:** minimal teacher input; students take initiative with available support
- **independent application:** full student ownership of learning processes.

This progression applies across all metacognitive strategies and should be adjusted based on individual student needs and the complexity of new skills being introduced.

2. Cross-curricular strategy transfer

Advanced students learn to apply metacognitive strategies across different subjects. A Year 6 student might recognise that the planning strategy used in writing can also help organise thinking for a science investigation.

'I use the same checking strategy in maths and science – I always ask myself, "Does this answer make sense?" In maths, if I get 150 when adding 6+7, I know something's wrong. In science, if my prediction seems impossible, I need to think again.'

Adapting for diverse needs: Apply the adaptation principles outlined in the 'Meeting diverse needs' section. For students with learning differences, explicitly teach how thinking strategies can transfer across subjects rather than assuming automatic transfer. For EAL students, help them recognise that strategies developed in their home language and culture can be applied in English academic contexts.

Internalising metacognitive strategies for lifelong learning

Having explored the four developmental stages of metacognitive growth, we now turn to the ultimate goal: supporting disadvantaged students in internalising these strategies for lifelong learning. This process – where students move from external guidance to self-directed metacognitive thinking – is especially important for those with fewer opportunities to develop these skills outside school.

Internalisation involves a gradual transition from explicit instruction to independent application. Vygotsky's (1978) concept of the Zone of Proximal Development underscores the value of scaffolding, where learners initially rely on support from teachers or peers before gradually taking ownership of their learning. This progression is reflected in the four developmental stages outlined earlier, moving systematically from foundational awareness to independent self-regulation.

Once internalised, metacognitive strategies yield long-term benefits that extend far beyond the classroom. Learners who adopt these approaches become more adaptable – an essential skill in today's fast-changing educational and professional landscapes. They can assess new situations, anticipate challenges and adjust their approaches accordingly. They also develop increased academic resilience, learning to persist through difficulties and view setbacks as opportunities rather than failures.

Perhaps most importantly, as students experience success through their own strategic thinking, their self-efficacy grows. This increased confidence in their ability to learn creates a positive cycle, encouraging them to tackle challenging tasks and assume greater ownership of their learning.

Key takeaways

- Metacognitive modelling plays a pivotal role in helping students internalise the thought processes that underpin deeper, more independent learning.
- When teachers make their thinking visible – explicitly demonstrating how they plan, connect ideas, monitor progress and evaluate their understanding – they provide students with a practical framework for managing their own learning.
- With consistent modelling over time, students begin to adopt and internalise these strategies, transitioning from reliance on external guidance to independently regulating their own thinking.

Reflection prompts

- Where are most of your students in their metacognitive development? What evidence do you see of their thinking awareness across different subjects?
- How often do you explicitly verbalise your thinking processes during lessons? Which subjects or activities might benefit from more think-aloud demonstrations?
- How do you adapt your modelling for students with different needs – including EAL learners, those with SEND or pupils experiencing disadvantage?
- In which areas could you help students recognise that thinking strategies transfer between subjects? What explicit connections could you make?

- How do you acknowledge and build upon the metacognitive practices students bring from their home cultures and languages?
- What signs of metacognitive growth do you look for? How do you celebrate thinking development alongside academic achievement?

Next steps

Metacognitive modelling is not an additional task – it's a way of making your existing high-quality teaching more visible and accessible to all learners.

Table 6: Implementing metacognitive modelling

Timeframe	Focus area	Actions
Week 1–2	Audit your current practice	• Start small and build systematically. • Record one lesson and count instances of explicit thinking. • Identify students with and without metacognitive awareness. • Select one subject area to enhance think-aloud modelling.
Week 3–4	Begin intentional modelling	• Choose three key thinking processes to model (e.g. predicting, checking, adjusting). • Use Stage 1 implementation with youngest or least metacognitively aware students. • Incorporate gesture and visual supports alongside verbal modelling.
Week 5–8	Expand and differentiate	• Embed subject-specific metacognitive moments across the curriculum. • Apply troubleshooting strategies for students not responding to initial approaches. • Create visual stage guides to track student progress.
Ongoing	Continued development	• Collaborate with colleagues to share effective modelling examples. • Document student progress using stage-specific indicators. • Plan support for transitions to the next developmental stage.

Preparing for structured implementation

While metacognitive modelling lays the groundwork for developing students' awareness of their thinking, many teachers benefit from a structured framework that breaks metacognitive processes into clear, manageable steps (Table 6). This is especially helpful when working with disadvantaged students, who often respond well to explicit routines and predictable learning structures.

The next chapter introduces the PCCME cycle: a systematic approach that builds on the modelling principles explored here. While this chapter has focused on making teacher thinking visible, the following chapter will demonstrate how to guide students through their own metacognitive processes using a consistent, repeatable framework.

5 PCCME: The blueprint for metacognitive learning

Metacognition is most powerful when it moves from theory into practice, especially for disadvantaged students who benefit from explicit routines and structured support. This chapter introduces a practical, step-by-step framework for teaching metacognitive skills in classrooms, with a focus on helping all learners become more independent, resilient and self-aware.

Building on the theoretical foundations from Chapter 2, the teacher-focused principles in Chapter 3 and the modelling strategies explored in Chapter 4, we now bring these elements together through the PCCME cycle: Plan, Connect, Check, Monitor, Evaluate. Each phase will be broken down and illustrated with practical strategies, teacher modelling techniques and real-life examples from schools across England. By the end of this chapter, you will have a clear, repeatable structure for guiding pupils through their own thinking processes, one that supports metacognitive development and helps close the gap for those facing significant barriers to learning.

The need for a structured approach

Supporting disadvantaged students demands strategic, structured and evidence-informed teaching that addresses the complex barriers they face. Despite sustained efforts, the attainment gap between disadvantaged pupils and their peers remains stubbornly wide. According to the Department for Education (2024), only 44 per cent of disadvantaged pupils achieved the expected standard in reading, writing and maths at Key Stage 2, compared to 66 per cent of all other pupils – a gap of 22 percentage points. This disparity equates to approximately 10.3 months of lost learning by age 11. The disadvantage gap index has risen to 3.13, compared with 2.91 in 2019. This means the learning gap between disadvantaged pupils and their peers is now wider than it was before the pandemic. In practical terms, disadvantaged pupils are, on average, further behind academically than they were five years ago (Education Policy Institute, 2024).

This gap cannot be closed solely through content delivery. It requires the explicit teaching of the thinking skills that underpin effective learning. Research consistently identifies metacognition as one of the most impactful strategies for improving student outcomes, particularly for those facing disadvantage (Education Endowment Foundation, 2018). The EEF rates metacognition and self-regulation as having 'very high impact for very low cost', with an average effect size equivalent to seven months' additional progress, making it one of the most cost-effective interventions available to schools (Education Endowment Foundation, 2021).

However, without a systematic approach, efforts to develop metacognitive skills risk being inconsistent and superficial. Dignath and Büttner's (2008) meta-analysis found that metacognitive instruction is most effective when it is deliberate, sustained and integrated across subjects rather than taught as isolated skills. This is where the structured blueprint becomes essential: it provides a coherent framework that teachers can implement consistently across year groups and subjects, ensuring that metacognitive development is embedded rather than incidental.

A systematic approach to thinking

To address the persistent attainment gap previously outlined, schools require a structured framework that enables all students to develop metacognitive skills in a consistent and meaningful way. The blueprint introduced in this chapter comprises five interconnected phases: Plan, Connect, Check, Monitor and Evaluate. These phases mirror the natural thinking processes of successful learners and provide a practical structure for embedding metacognition across the curriculum.

Developed through extensive classroom practice in primary schools across England – from inner-city schools in London to rural primaries in Yorkshire – the PCCME cycle emerged in response to teachers' need for a systematic approach to developing metacognitive skills in students who had not acquired them naturally. Each phase builds upon the previous, creating a cumulative learning process that students can internalise and apply across subjects.

Importantly, the framework addresses the 'hidden curriculum' – the unspoken rules and strategies that advantaged students often absorb through home environments and informal learning (Bourdieu & Passeron, 1990). By making these invisible processes explicit and teachable, the blueprint helps level the playing field for students who are disadvantaged.

Each phase serves a distinct purpose:

- **Plan:** setting clear learning goals and selecting appropriate strategies before beginning a task. This phase is important for pupils eligible for free school meals, who may come from homes where structured planning is not modelled (Hart & Risley, 1995). Rather than diving straight into tasks, students learn to pause and consider their approach, developing the executive function skills that are often underdeveloped in disadvantaged learners (Moffitt et al., 2011).

- **Connect:** linking new learning to prior knowledge and experiences. This phase helps students build cognitive bridges that make new information meaningful and memorable (Ausubel, 1968). For disadvantaged students, whose out-of-school experiences may differ from middle-class assumptions embedded in curriculum content (Heath, 1983), explicit connection-making ensures equitable access to learning.

- **Check:** establishing and understanding success criteria. This phase transforms vague expectations into concrete targets, enabling students to assess their own progress and navigate academic tasks with greater clarity (Bernstein, 1971).

- **Monitor:** tracking progress and adjusting strategies during learning. This phase develops self-awareness and agency, particularly for students who may have internalised learned helplessness through repeated academic struggles (Seligman, 1972).

- **Evaluate:** reflecting on learning outcomes and planning for future improvement. This phase fosters the growth mindset that research indicates is crucial for overcoming the effects of disadvantage (Dweck, 2006; Yeager & Dweck, 2012).

Together, these phases transform the metacognitive modelling discussed in Chapter 4 into a systematic routine that students can apply independently across their learning experiences. The PCCME cycle is not simply a teaching tool – it is a pedagogical approach that fosters independence, resilience and self-belief.

Plan: Setting purpose and preparing for learning

Why it matters

Disadvantaged students often lack exposure to structured planning at home. The Plan phase teaches them to pause, set goals and choose strategies – developing executive function and agency. This section examines how teachers can explicitly teach planning skills, providing practical strategies and adaptations to address common barriers.

Table 7: Characteristics of the Plan stage

Key characteristics	Teacher's role	Signs of progress
• Setting clear learning goals and intentions • Selecting appropriate strategies before beginning • Anticipating potential challenges • Organising resources and approach	• Model planning through think-alouds • Provide planning templates and scaffolds • Guide students in breaking tasks into steps • Ask prompting questions about approach	• Student pauses before starting work • Student articulates goals and strategies • Student prepares materials thoughtfully • Student connects task to previous learning

Mr Davies, a Year 10 teacher in Birmingham, observed that pupils were overwhelmed by independent research tasks, often waiting passively for instructions: 'They didn't know where to start and would wait for step-by-step instructions instead of trying things for themselves.' In a school where nearly 70 per cent of pupils qualify for free school meals, this pattern reflects a broader issue: many students come from households where academic planning is not routinely modelled or supported.

The Plan phase addresses this gap by making the invisible process of preparation explicit and routine (Table 7). Rather than assuming students know how to approach learning, teachers teach and model the planning systematically until it becomes second nature. For disadvantaged students, this is not just helpful – it's essential. It compensates for the 'cultural capital' that middle-class students often acquire through family conversations about goals, strategies and problem-solving (Bourdieu, 1986).

Understanding the planning process

The planning process begins with three fundamental questions that transform passive students into strategic learners:

- **What am I trying to achieve?** This clarifies purpose and encourages goal-setting rather than working aimlessly – particularly important for students whose home environments may lack goal-oriented conversations (Lareau, 2003).
- **What strategies will help me?** This builds strategic thinking, helping students move beyond guesswork and towards intentional learning.
- **What challenges might I face, and how can I overcome them?** Fosters resilience and forward-thinking, addressing the learned helplessness that can develop in students who face repeated academic struggles (Seligman, 1972).

At a primary school in Birmingham, where 78 per cent of pupils are eligible for free school meals and 45 per cent have English as an additional language, Year 4 teacher Mr Singh noticed dramatic changes when he introduced these planning questions. 'Before, if students got stuck, they'd either put their hands up immediately or just stop working,' he explains. 'Now they pause and ask themselves what else they could try. It's transformed their resilience, particularly for my pupils who used to see struggle as evidence they couldn't do it.'

These kinds of planning questions are powerful, but they are harder to apply due to distinct barriers disadvantaged students face. Language, confidence and continuity issues frequently intersect, requiring targeted, systematic support (Sutton Trust, 2019). Table 8 provides guidance on how to adapt strategies to target specific challenges.

Table 8: Adaptation guidelines

Student challenge	Specific barrier	Support
English as additional language	Limited vocabulary prevents task comprehension	Use visual planning templates with dual-language support; model task breakdown aloud; encourage identification of difficult parts and planning for support
Housing instability	Learning gaps undermine confidence to plan	Provide knowledge organisers for quick recaps; prompt reflection on missed content; set realistic, step-by-step goals

Student challenge	Specific barrier	Support
Low literacy levels	Reading/writing difficulties obscure instructions	Use oral planning discussions; model non-text planning approaches; support visual/verbal task clarification
Emotional/behavioural challenges	Anxiety and low focus hinder task initiation	Create predictable planning routines; teach emotional regulation alongside planning; encourage positive self-talk
Limited home support	Lack of planning habit development	Make planning explicit and repetitive; model planning questions; allow peer discussion time

Metacognitive moment: Making thinking visible for EAL learners

At her primary school in Tower Hamlets, where 89 per cent of pupils speak English as an additional language, Year 3 teacher Ms Ahmed uses a structured, research-informed approach to planning. She uses visual planning templates with key vocabulary in both English and heritage languages, provides dual-language sentence starters, and models breaking down tasks aloud: *'What do I already know about this topic – in my first language or in English?'* (Conteh, 2015).

'Before, my EAL pupils would nod and smile but often hadn't understood what they were supposed to do. Now they can articulate their goals clearly and know what support to seek when they need it.'

This aligns with Strand and Demie's (2005) findings that EAL pupils benefit from explicit vocabulary support to access task instructions and prior knowledge.

Students affected by housing instability often struggle to link new content to prior knowledge due to disrupted learning. At Nevermore Secondary School in Manchester, where student mobility exceeds the national average, Year 9 teacher Ms Sharif uses a 'learning passport' system to support high-mobility learners. Drawing on research by Dobson and Henthorne (1999), she gives pupils 'knowledge organisers' covering key topics in science and history, helping them catch up on learning they have missed. She also works with them to set realistic, achievable goals, which in turn help pupils rebuild both continuity and confidence, even when their education has been disrupted.

Common challenges and solutions in the Plan phase

While the Plan phase is foundational for clarity and direction, many learners struggle to engage effectively with this phase. Teachers often observe confusion, hesitation or rushed starts – symptoms of deeper barriers, such as unclear expectations, limited prior knowledge or low confidence.

Challenge 1: Difficulty understanding the task

Students often begin tasks without fully grasping what is expected, leading to misdirected or unfocused work.

Solutions

- **Model task unpacking** through think-alouds to demonstrate how to analyse a task: *'Let's break this question down – what is it asking me to do first?'*
- **Rephrase tasks** in plain language or use icons and images.
- **Use planning prompts** such as sentence starters: *'My task is to...'* or *'I will need to...'*.

Challenge 2: Limited prior knowledge or experience

Students may struggle to plan because they don't know what they already know – or mistakenly believe they know nothing.

Solutions

- **Activate prior knowledge** with retrieval activities, mind maps or discussion to surface existing understanding.
- **Use knowledge organisers or anchor charts** to help students make connections.
- **Prompt reflection**, for example *'Have I done anything like this before? What worked well last time?'*.

Quick strategy guide: Learning launch

- A structured five-minute planning routine at the start of significant learning activities can help embed metacognitive habits without overwhelming students. This short routine maintains engagement even for students with attention difficulties and is substantial enough to build genuine planning habits.

- Teachers present learning objectives using child-friendly language and visual supports, demonstrating that clarity of purpose is crucial for student engagement (Hattie, 2009).

- They model setting specific, measurable goals while thinking aloud (Vygotsky, 1978).

- Students receive sentence starters such as *'Today I will...'* and *'I will know I've succeeded when...'* which scaffold thinking without overwhelming cognitive load.

- For students struggling with open-ended goal-setting, teachers provide choices between 2–3 pre-written goals at different challenge levels, ensuring success while developing decision-making skills (Katz & Assor, 2007).

Connect: Activating prior knowledge and building bridges

The Connect phase tackles a persistent challenge: helping all students access learning, regardless of prior knowledge and experiences. Vocabulary gaps between advantaged and disadvantaged children are evident by age three and continue to widen throughout primary school, significantly impacting comprehension across all subjects (Sutton Trust, 2010).

Miss Roberts, a Year 1 teacher at Oakwood Primary in Leeds, was halfway through a topic on families when she realised she'd made an assumption. 'I'd planned around the idea of a typical nuclear family', she says, 'but my class was anything but typical – some kids lived with one parent, some with grandparents, some were in foster care, and others had big extended families. It made me rethink how I taught it. That mix wasn't a problem – it was something we could learn from.'

This reflects the concept of 'funds of knowledge', developed by González et al. (2005), which is the idea that all students bring valuable experiences from home and community contexts that can enrich learning when recognised and used.

The science of connection-making

Making connections is fundamental to how learning occurs, but disadvantaged students often lack the background knowledge that makes this process automatic. New information must be linked to existing knowledge to be understood and retained (van Kesteren et al., 2018). Assuming that all students bring similar prior knowledge perpetuates educational disadvantage in UK schools (Gorard & See, 2013).

The Connect phase makes this process explicit and inclusive, helping students surface and utilise the knowledge they already possess. Rather than privileging only curriculum-aligned or culturally dominant experiences, it encourages students to identify and use whatever relevant knowledge they bring, whether from home, community or lived experience. Teachers can support connection-making by prompting students to draw on diverse experiences: *'Have you seen something like this before – at home, in your community or in another country?'* This phrasing explicitly includes experiences that might not fit traditional expectations.

Creating emotional readiness for learning

Emotional readiness is often a hidden barrier to learning, particularly for disadvantaged pupils who may experience adverse childhood experiences, family stress or trauma. As many as two-thirds of children undergo at least one significant traumatic experience (Trivedi & Harrison, 2022), which can affect their ability to learn.

At Willowbrook Primary in Manchester, teachers begin lessons with short 'settling' routines: mood check-ins using emoji cards, mindfulness moments to help regulate stress responses and circle time to build community and belonging. These approaches reflect trauma-informed pedagogy research, which emphasises emotional regulation as a prerequisite for learning (Perry & Szalavitz, 2006). Further discussion on the link between mental wellbeing and its impact on education outcomes are covered in Chapter 9.

Common challenges and solutions in the Connect phase

Challenge 1: Limited background knowledge or vocabulary

A limited vocabulary of background knowledge may cause some students to struggle.

Solution

- Build a class knowledge bank of key concepts and vocabulary.
- Use visual supports (e.g. images, diagrams) to reinforce verbal explanations.
- Encourage structured peer dialogue where students can share their own connections.

Challenge 2: Surface-level connections

Some students might tend towards making surface-level connections with the work.

Solution

- Model deeper connection-making using because statements: *'This connects to... because...'*.
- Use prompts that push thinking, such as: *'How does this help you understand?'* or *'What does this connection tell you?'*.

Challenge 3: Pupils feeling their experience isn't relevant

If students don't see their reality modelled in discussions or examples, they may feel their experiences aren't relevant.

Solutions

- Explicitly validate diverse forms of knowledge and experience.
- Show how everyday experiences connect to academic concepts.

Check: Defining success and building clarity

The Check phase addresses a key equity issue: the 'hidden curriculum' of expectations that advantaged students often absorb informally, while disadvantaged students are left to decode them without support. Bernstein (1971) demonstrated how middle-class students benefit from implicit familiarity with educational codes and expectations, while working-class students face barriers in understanding what schools actually want from them.

At Valley Primary in Wales, Year 5 teacher Mr Davies observed that pupils whose parents had attended university seemed to instinctively understand what made a 'good' piece of writing – tone, structure and depth – while equally capable students from working-class backgrounds met the basic requirements but missed the unstated expectations.

Making success tangible

The Check phase centres on a powerful question that transforms vague expectations into concrete targets: *'What does success look like in this task?'* This question is particularly important for disadvantaged students, who may not have developed the ability to decode implicit academic expectations through home experiences (Heath, 1983).

Clarity of learning intentions and success criteria can significantly improve student outcomes – Hattie (2009) reports an effect size of 0.48, equivalent to 5–6 months of additional progress, making it one of the most impactful teaching strategies available. This means that when teachers clearly communicate *what students are expected to learn* (learning intentions) and *how they will know they've succeeded* (success criteria), it can have a substantial positive effect on student learning.

- **Effect size of 0.48:** In Hattie's framework, an effect size measures the impact of a teaching strategy on student learning. An effect size of 0.4 or above is considered 'highly effective', so 0.48 is well above average.

- **Equivalent to 5–6 months of additional progress:** This translates the effect size into a practical measure – students can achieve roughly half a year's extra learning over a school year compared to if the strategy wasn't used.

- **Impact:** Because of this strong effect, making learning intentions and success criteria clear is considered one of the most powerful strategies a teacher can use to improve student outcomes.

In short, it emphasises that clarity and transparency in teaching goals directly accelerate learning.

According to Hattie (2009), clarity of learning intentions and success criteria is particularly important for a number of reasons:

- **Focuses student attention:** When students know exactly what they are expected to learn, they can concentrate their effort on the key goals rather than guessing what matters.
- **Guides self-assessment:** Success criteria give students a concrete way to measure their own progress. They can check whether they are on track and adjust their approach if needed.
- **Supports feedback:** Clear goals allow teachers to give more targeted feedback, and students can interpret feedback more effectively because it's tied to specific learning outcomes.
- **Promotes metacognition:** Students learn to plan, monitor and evaluate their learning strategies, building independence and self-regulation.
- **Reduces confusion and anxiety:** Uncertainty about expectations can slow learning; clarity removes that barrier, making learning more efficient.

In essence, it works because it turns vague tasks into *transparent, measurable, and actionable learning experiences*, which accelerates progress.

At St. Michael's Primary in Liverpool, where 89 per cent of pupils receive free school meals, Year 2 teacher Mrs O'Brien has revolutionised her approach to success criteria. 'I used to say things like 'write a story' and assume children knew what that meant', she explains. 'Now we co-construct what makes a good story: characters the reader cares about, a problem that gets solved, interesting describing words and sentences that make sense when read aloud.'

Common challenges and solutions in the Check phase

Challenge 1: Inaccurate self-assessment

Learners often struggle to judge their understanding or strategy effectiveness objectively. This may be due to overestimating competence or not knowing which indicators to use, which undermines the Check phase.

Challenge 2: Lack of specific criteria

Without clear learning goals or success criteria established in the Plan phase, learners can't tell whether they are on track, leading to superficial or inconsistent evaluation.

Solution

- Explicit success criteria: Define clear, measurable indicators of progress at the start so learners know what to check against (e.g. mastery targets, rubric benchmarks).

Challenge 3: Cognitive load and distraction

Under pressure, learners may skip reflective checks or default to familiar but ineffective strategies rather than examining real performance data.

Solution

- Structured self-questioning prompts: Tools such as reflective checklists or guided questions (e.g. *'What worked?'*, *'What didn't?'*) help learners focus the Check phase on evidence rather than impression.

Challenge 4: Emotional barriers

Frustration or anxiety about performance can cause avoidance of honest self-assessment, especially if feedback is perceived as negative.

Solutions

- Training in self-assessment and feedback interpretation: Teachers can model how to interpret external feedback, teaching learners how to calibrate their judgements against objective measures.
- Regular micro-reflection pauses: Encourage brief, scheduled pauses during tasks to check understanding and adjust strategies in real time rather than deferring reflection only to the end.

Quick guide

To support the Check phase, teachers must move beyond stating objectives and instead discuss success criteria with students. This can include:

- **Modelling what success looks like** through exemplar work and annotated samples.
- **Collaborative generation of criteria**, encouraging students to suggest what a strong answer or product would include.
- **Visual displays or reference tools**, such as checklists, rubrics or sentence stems.
- **Verbal reinforcement** during lessons, using phrases like *'Remember, our goal is...'* or *'Let's check if we're meeting our success criteria...'*.

Such strategies help make success tangible. This is especially important for disadvantaged pupils who may not instinctively grasp what is expected or how to reach high standards due to limited exposure to academic language or high-performing models.

Monitor: Tracking progress and maintaining focus

The Monitor phase addresses one of the most significant challenges facing disadvantaged students: developing the self-regulation skills necessary to remain engaged in learning. Self-control in childhood is a powerful predictor of adult outcomes (Moffitt et al., 2011), but students from disadvantaged backgrounds often have fewer opportunities to develop these crucial capabilities. At Greenfield Primary in Tower Hamlets, Year 3 teacher Mrs Ahmed observed that while some pupils worked steadily and adjusted their approach, others – often those facing challenges at home – rushed through tasks or gave up quickly.

Self-monitoring involves the continuous process of checking understanding, tracking progress and maintaining focus during learning. As discussed in Chapter 2, Flavell (1979) identified monitoring as essential for self-regulated learning; however, disadvantaged students often require explicit instruction and systematic support to develop this skill.

Monitoring involves asking: *'How am I doing right now? Do I understand what I'm learning? Is my current approach working? What should I do if I'm struggling?'* These questions may seem simple, but they reflect sophisticated metacognitive processes that many disadvantaged students haven't had opportunities to develop (Zimmerman, 2002). At Riverside Secondary in Manchester, where many students have experienced adverse childhood events, Year 9 teacher Ms Smith has developed monitoring approaches that recognise these realities. 'I used to assume students would naturally notice when they were confused or struggling', she reflects. 'Now I understand that for some pupils, coping with stress or instability can take priority over noticing gaps in understanding. We have to explicitly teach them to tune into their own thinking and monitor their learning.'

Developing strategic monitoring tools

One of the most effective approaches involves teaching students to use concrete tools that support their monitoring processes. These tools help make abstract thinking visible and manageable – especially for those with executive function challenges.

- **Monitoring bookmarks** are key questions students can ask themselves during independent work: *'Do I understand what I'm doing? Am I following my plan? Do I need to change my approach?'* These physical prompts help students who might otherwise forget to monitor their thinking regularly.

- **Self-check pauses** every 10–15 minutes during extended work periods give teachers a chance to signal brief reflection moments for students to assess their progress and make necessary adjustments. This regularity helps students develop internal monitoring rhythms.

- **Traffic light systems** (e.g. green = confident, amber = unsure, red = stuck) help students assess and respond to their understanding. This system works because it normalises different levels of understanding while providing clear signals for appropriate responses.

Adjusting strategies is part of monitoring – not a separate phase. When students notice something isn't working, they learn to respond and adapt.

Common challenges and solutions in the Monitor phase

The Monitor phase involves students checking their understanding, tracking their progress, and assessing whether their current strategies are effective *as they work*. This is crucial for staying on course, catching mistakes early and making real-time adjustments. However, many learners struggle to monitor their own thinking and performance. The following challenges and solutions reflect common classroom patterns and offer practical ways to support metacognitive development.

Challenge 1: Continuous work

Students work through a task without pausing to assess their understanding.

Solutions

- Introduce learning pit stops: Build in pauses where students reflect using questions like *'Is this making sense?'* or *'Am I following my plan?'*.

- Use visual cues: Display metacognitive prompts such as *'What am I doing well?'* or *'What's confusing me?'*.

- Model self-checking aloud: Demonstrate your own in-the-moment thinking, e.g. *'Hmm, I'm not sure that answer makes sense – let me go back and check.'*

Challenge 2: Assumption of accuracy without verification

Students assume they're doing well without verifying accuracy or their understanding. This is especially common among those with inconsistent academic confidence.

Solutions

- Use *success criteria checklists*: Provide a simple visual or written guide students can tick off as they work.

- Encourage *peer questioning*: Pair students to ask each other questions like *'Have you answered all parts of the task?'* or *'Can you explain what you've done so far?'*.

- Praise *accuracy and perseverance over speed*: Reinforce the value of thoughtful work and self-correction rather than early completion.

Evaluate: Reflecting on learning and planning ahead

This phase helps students reflect on their learning and plan what to do differently next time. For disadvantaged students, this phase provides a structured opportunity to assess their progress, identify strengths and weaknesses, and build the confidence to move forward.

The power of reflection

Reflection encourages students to think critically about what they have learned, how they approached tasks and whether their strategies worked. This self-assessment helps students link effort to outcome – particularly important for disadvantaged learners, who may not yet see themselves as capable or in control of their learning.

However, reflection isn't just about celebrating success; it also involves identifying areas where improvement is needed. Teachers can facilitate this by providing guiding questions such as: *'What worked well during this task?'* and *'What would you do differently next time?'*. These encourage students to think critically about their learning while staying focused on improvement.

Planning for future learning

After reflecting, students can plan what to do differently next time. This forward-looking aspect encourages students to view challenges as opportunities for improvement rather than insurmountable obstacles.

Planning ahead means setting realistic goals, identifying strategies to overcome obstacles, and determining how to approach future tasks more effectively. For example, a student who struggles with time management might break tasks into smaller steps or set specific deadlines to stay on track, building the self-regulation skills that support long-term academic success (Zimmerman, 2002).

Common challenges and solutions in the Evaluate phase

The Evaluate phase is where students reflect on how well they completed a task, the effectiveness of the strategies they used, and what they might do differently next time. It is vital for closing the learning loop and building a deeper understanding, but disadvantaged learners often need explicit support to engage meaningfully in this stage. Below are common challenges and targeted solutions to help embed evaluation into everyday practice.

Challenge 1: Superficial or vague reflections

Students may say things like 'It was fine' or 'I did OK' without explaining any specifics of what happened.

Solutions

- Use guided reflection prompts such as: *'One thing that worked well was...', 'Next time I would try...', 'A strategy I used was... and it helped me because...'*
- Model deeper reflection, e.g. *'I rushed through the planning and that made my final answer unclear. Next time I'll slow down.'*

Challenge 2: Difficulty linking outcome to strategy

An absence of reflection often means students struggle to see how their strategy results in an outcome.

Solutions

- Use class discussions to unpack what led to success or difficulty: *'How did the plan we used affect the results we got?'*
- Create strategy trackers where students tick off strategies used and then reflect on which ones were effective.
- Compare different approaches using peer examples.

Classroom snapshot: The PCCME cycle in action

Many Year 10 pupils at Brookside Secondary have experienced disrupted learning. To support them, the PCCME cycle is applied deliberately across a multi-lesson chemistry investigation exploring factors affecting the rate of reaction between hydrochloric acid and magnesium. Students are encouraged to combine metacognitive strategies with analytical reasoning.

1   **Plan:** Students begin by completing a 'Project Planner' template, identifying their research question, variables and equipment. Liam, who struggles with organisation, works with Ms Johnson to sequence steps and justify his choices: *'Why am I changing the concentration of the acid rather than the surface area of magnesium? How will that give me clearer insights into the reaction rate?'*

2   **Connect:** The class participates in a 'Knowledge Harvest', recalling prior learning on collision theory, particle movement and rates of reaction. Aisha, who recently joined the school, links concepts from her previous lessons with everyday observations (e.g. effervescence in fizzy drinks). Students evaluate which prior knowledge is reliable and relevant.

3   **Check:** Ms Johnson co-creates success criteria with the class, emphasising accuracy, control of variables and the ability to justify conclusions. She prompts: *'How will you ensure your results are accurate? What trends should you expect, and why? How can you interpret anomalies?'* Laminated checklists help students assess each step and reflect on their choices.

4   **Monitor:** Midway through the experiment, students complete a 'Progress Check' form: *'What's working well? Are my measurements consistent? Do I notice unexpected results? How might I improve my procedure?'* Marcus, who often rushes, notices his gas collection is inconsistent. He adjusts by repeating trials and refining his timing, demonstrating metacognitive monitoring and critical evaluation.

5   **Evaluate:** After the investigation, students use a structured protocol to evaluate their data, reasoning and conclusions. Class discussions focus on assessing design choices, sources of error and alternative explanations, highlighting how metacognition and critical thinking deepens understanding of chemical reactions.

This structured approach transforms a potentially overwhelming task into a manageable and empowering learning experience, particularly for students who might otherwise struggle with complex, extended assignments.

Quick strategy guides

Goal-setting

Time required: Five minutes at the start of the lesson, 2–3 minutes for mid-lesson check-in and end-of-lesson reflection

Preparation: Prepare visual goal templates with differentiated examples

Steps:

1 Present the learning objective and explain its importance.

2 Model a specific, measurable goal linked to the objective.

3 Provide sentence starters to scaffold thinking: *'Today I will...', 'I will know I've succeeded when...'.*

4 For students who need support, offer a choice of 2–3 pre-written goals.

5 Ask students to record their goal visibly (on desks, in books or on shared displays).

6 Mid-lesson, check progress using a quick thumbs up/middle/down or similar visual signal.

7 End with brief reflection: *'Did I meet my goal? What helped/got in the way?'*

Implementation notes:

• Include confidence goals alongside academic ones.

• Normalise goal adjustment as part of learning – not as a sign of failure.

• Use visual symbols or colour-coding to support younger pupils and those with EAL.

Adaptation guideline: PCCME for specific disadvantages

For students with limited English proficiency

• Plan: Provide visual planning templates with dual language support.

• Connect: Use images and real objects to bridge language gaps.

• Check: Create visual success criteria with minimal text.

• Monitor: Offer non-verbal monitoring signals (traffic light cards).

• Evaluate: Allow reflection through drawing or L1 writing (writing in a pupil's native language) initially.

For students with inconsistent attendance

- Plan: Create planning routines that include quick refreshers.
- Connect: Maintain personal 'learning maps' showing connections between lessons.
- Check: Provide consistent success criteria formats across lessons.
- Monitor: Teach self-monitoring strategies that don't rely on a teacher's presence.
- Evaluate: Use structured templates that scaffold reflection independently.

For students with emotional/behavioural challenges

- Plan: Include emotional readiness in planning ('How am I feeling about this task?').
- Connect: Acknowledge emotional connections to learning topics.
- Check: Break success criteria into smaller, achievable chunks.
- Monitor: Embed emotional check-ins alongside cognitive monitoring.
- Evaluate: Celebrate effort and strategy use, not just outcomes.

Starting small: A phased approach

Rather than implementing the entire PCCME cycle immediately, successful schools begin with a single phase that addresses their students' most pressing needs, allowing both teachers and students to develop confidence and competence without feeling overwhelmed.

- **Phase 1 Focus (Weeks 1–4):** If students struggle to begin tasks confidently, start with strengthening the Plan phase through consistent five-minute learning launches and goal-setting routines.
- **Phase 2 Integration (Weeks 5–8):** Once planning becomes routine, add the Connect phase by explicitly teaching connection-making strategies and validating diverse student experiences.
- **Phase 3 Expansion (Weeks 9–12):** Introduce the Check phase by co-constructing success criteria and making expectations transparent.
- **Phase 4 Development (Weeks 13–16):** Add systematic monitoring through regular self-check pauses and progress tracking tools.
- **Phase 5 Completion (Weeks 17–20):** Implement structured evaluation and reflection routines that close the learning loop.

Cross-curricular applications

The PCCME cycle's power lies in its adaptability across subjects. In Mrs Ahmed's Year 5 science lessons, students investigate 'Which materials are the best thermal insulators?' using the complete cycle:

- **Plan** by identifying their research question and selecting appropriate methods.
- **Connect** by discussing prior knowledge about heat and insulation from everyday life.
- **Check** by establishing success criteria for a good scientific investigation.
- **Monitor** their method during the experiment and adjust if needed.
- **Evaluate** their findings against predictions while planning improvements for future investigations.

This cross-curricular application helps disadvantaged students recognise that thinking strategies transfer between subjects, building the strategic flexibility that is crucial for academic success (Dignath & Büttner, 2008).

Assessment and progress tracking

Teachers can track PCCME impact using three types of evidence:

- **Observational evidence** includes students pausing before starting tasks, asking clarifying questions about success criteria, self-correcting independently and using metacognitive language naturally.
- **Student work evidence** shows planning notes that demonstrate thoughtful preparation, work that demonstrates strategic thinking and self-assessments that show accurate self-awareness.
- **Engagement indicators** include increased persistence when facing challenges, students seeking appropriate help when needed, and improved ability to transfer strategies across subjects.

For disadvantaged students, progress might be evidenced by increased participation, improved self-advocacy and greater emotional regulation during challenging tasks – outcomes that have implications far beyond academic achievement.

Implementation checkpoint: PCCME cycle integration

Rate your current practice on the following aspects (1–5 scale, where 1 = not yet implemented and 5 = fully integrated):

1 I have clear routines for each phase of the PCCME cycle.

2 I provide appropriate scaffolding for disadvantaged students during each phase.

3 I consistently model metacognitive thinking related to each phase.

4 My students can articulate which phase of the cycle they're in and why it matters.

5 I see evidence of students independently applying elements of the cycle.

Next steps

- If you scored mostly 1–2: Focus on implementing one phase thoroughly before adding others.
- If you scored mostly 3: Work on smoother transitions between phases and more consistent application.
- If you scored mostly 4–5: Begin reducing scaffolding to promote greater independence.

One-week challenge

Choose one curriculum area and implement the complete PCCME cycle for a single lesson or unit. Document the impact on disadvantaged students specifically, noting changes in engagement, persistence and strategic thinking.

The role of the teacher

For this blueprint to be effective, teachers must model metacognitive thinking consistently, scaffold each phase appropriately, and create a classroom culture that values reflection, curiosity and emotional safety. This requires professional reflection, collaboration and leadership support to embed the framework into wider school systems.

Teachers should view the blueprint not as an 'add-on' but as core pedagogy that enhances every subject area. With planning and shared practice, the cycle becomes a natural part of daily instruction, helping to close attainment gaps by giving all students access to high-level thinking skills.

Creating a metacognitive classroom environment

A metacognitive classroom is characterised by visible thinking routines, reflective dialogue and a growth mindset culture. Physical displays show thinking strategies, success criteria are co-constructed and visible, and students' metacognitive language is celebrated and developed.

Mistakes are reframed as learning opportunities, students regularly share their thinking processes, and there's dedicated time for reflection and planning. This environment provides the psychological safety and structure disadvantaged students need to take risks and grow as learners.

Classroom snapshot: Growth mindset language

Mrs Begum noticed pupils frequently saying 'I can't do this' or 'I'm rubbish at maths'. She realised these fixed-mindset statements revealed not just low confidence but poor metacognitive awareness – pupils didn't recognise that struggle is part of learning and that strategies can help.

She introduced 'power phrases' that combined growth mindset with metacognitive strategies:

- Instead of 'I can't do this' → 'I can't do this yet. What strategy could help?'
- Instead of 'I'm rubbish at maths' → 'This type of problem is tricky for me. What do I need to focus on?'
- Instead of 'It's too hard' → 'This is challenging. Should I break it into steps or ask for help?'

She displayed these phrases prominently and modelled using them herself. When pupils used fixed-mindset language, she'd gently redirect.

Over time, pupils internalised these phrases. Their language shifted from helpless to strategic, which improved both their wellbeing and their learning outcomes.

Building independence through gradual release

The ultimate goal of the PCCME cycle is student independence. This requires careful scaffolding and gradual release of responsibility.

Initial stage (teacher-led)

- Teacher models each phase explicitly.
- Students observe and discuss the thinking processes.
- Whole-class practice with significant guidance.

Developing stage (guided practice)

- Students work in pairs or small groups.
- Teacher provides structured templates and prompts.
- Regular check-ins and feedback.

Consolidating stage (independent practice)

- Students apply the cycle with minimal scaffolding.
- Self-assessment becomes routine.
- Peer support replaces teacher guidance.

Mastery stage (transfer and adaptation)

- Students adapt the cycle to new contexts.
- They teach others and explain their thinking.
- Metacognitive habits are internalised.

For disadvantaged students, this progression may take longer and require additional support at each stage. However, the investment pays dividends in increased independence and confidence.

How to know the blueprint is working

Teachers can track the effectiveness of the PCCME cycle through various indicators as outlined in Table 9.

Table 9: Tracking the PCCME cycle

Type of evidence	Indicators
Observational evidence	• Students pause before starting tasks. • They ask clarifying questions about success criteria. • They self-correct and adjust strategies independently. • They use metacognitive language naturally.
Student work evidence	• Planning notes show thoughtful preparation. • Work demonstrates strategic thinking. • Students identify and explain their problem-solving approaches. • Self-assessments show accurate self-awareness.
Engagement indicators	• Increased persistence is shown when facing challenges. • Students seek appropriate help when needed. • Greater confidence is shown in approaching new tasks. • There is an improved ability to transfer strategies across subjects.

For disadvantaged students, progress might be evidenced by increased participation, improved self-advocacy, and greater emotional regulation during challenging tasks – outcomes that have implications far beyond academic achievement.

Key takeaways

- The PCCME cycle provides a structured approach to improving outcomes for disadvantaged students.
- By explicitly teaching planning, connecting, checking, monitoring and evaluating, it transforms how students engage with tasks and understand their own learning.
- Where this blueprint is consistently applied, students develop metacognitive habits that drive success throughout life, offering a path to independence, confidence and long-term achievement that transcends many barriers they face.

Next steps

Start small: consistency in one area often yields better results than sporadic implementation of the entire framework. The investment in building these habits pays dividends in increased student agency, improved academic outcome, and in the lifelong learning skills that serve students well beyond their school years.

6 Making metacognition explicit

Metacognition isn't automatic – it must be taught. For disadvantaged students who may not have developed strategic learning habits at home, explicit instruction in how to plan, monitor and evaluate their thinking is essential.

This chapter focuses on how teachers can make metacognition visible and actionable in everyday lessons – through retrieval practice, analogies, scaffolding and reflection. These strategies help learners surface their thinking, build confidence and take ownership of their learning journey.

While previous chapters explored how teachers model metacognitive thinking and embed it through structured frameworks, this chapter focuses on making individual strategies explicit – so that students not only observe thinking but practise it deliberately. These approaches help surface invisible processes and equip learners with tools they can use independently.

Why explicit metacognitive instruction matters

Disadvantaged students face barriers that their peers do not. Limited access to books, educational resources and enrichment experiences means that they often arrive at school without the background knowledge or learning strategies others take for granted. They may have fewer opportunities to discuss learning at home, less exposure to academic vocabulary and limited experience with self-directed study.

This is where explicit metacognitive instruction becomes transformative. When teachers deliberately model and teach strategies for planning, monitoring and evaluating learning, they level the playing field. These approaches do not just close gaps in knowledge – they build the thinking skills that disadvantaged students need to become independent, resilient learners who can advocate for themselves and direct their own progress.

Practical strategies for making metacognition explicit

Strategy 1: Retrieval practice

Retrieval practice – actively recalling information from memory rather than passively reviewing notes – is one of the most powerful learning strategies we can teach. This process strengthens retention, promotes self-assessment and deepens understanding.

Research summary: Retrieval practice

- Study: Karpicke and Roediger (2008) The Critical Importance of Retrieval for Learning.
- Study focus: Comparing retrieval practice to repeated studying for long-term retention.
- Key finding: College students learning Swahili-English word pairs showed significantly better long-term retention when they practised retrieval (testing themselves) compared to repeated studying of the same material. The act of recalling information from memory strengthened the memory trace more effectively than passive review.
- Practical implication: Regular low-stakes testing is not just about assessment – it is a powerful learning tool. For disadvantaged students who may lack quiet study spaces or parental homework support, classroom-based retrieval practice provides essential memory strengthening that doesn't depend on home circumstances. Teachers should embed retrieval opportunities into every lesson.

For disadvantaged students, retrieval practice offers something crucial: a classroom-based strategy that is not reliant on resources at home. Bjork and Bjork (2011, p. 4) describe these as 'desirable difficulties' – challenges that make learning harder in the moment but deeper and more durable in the long run.

A Year 8 example: In an urban school with high levels of disadvantage, a science teacher introduced daily 'quiz games' at the start of each lesson.

Students recalled facts from previous lessons in a friendly competition format that reduced fear of failure. Over the term, the teacher observed significant improvements in both retention and students' ability to apply concepts in new contexts. Crucially, students began to self-assess – identifying gaps in their own knowledge and asking for targeted help.

Strategy 2: Using analogies to bridge knowledge gaps

Analogies are bridges – they connect unfamiliar concepts to known experiences, making abstract ideas concrete and memorable. For students who lack prior exposure to academic content, analogies provide cognitive scaffolding that compensates for earlier gaps.

Gentner's (1983) research on Structure-Mapping Theory shows that effective analogies highlight deep structural relationships between domains, not just surface similarities. When we compare an atom to a solar system, we're mapping relationships: electrons orbit the nucleus just as planets orbit the sun. This kind of relational thinking develops critical analysis and transfer skills.

What it looks like in practice:

- explaining the circulatory system as a city's transport network
- comparing electric circuits to water flowing through pipes
- relating poetic metaphor to everyday comparisons students already make
- asking students to generate their own analogies for new concepts.

Classroom snapshot

Students struggling with the abstract concept of photosynthesis connected it to cooking: plants use sunlight as 'energy' (like heat from a cooker), combine water and carbon dioxide as 'ingredients', and produce glucose (the 'meal') and oxygen (the 'steam'). This everyday analogy helped students visualise the process and retain the concept far better than textbook definitions alone.

Strategy 3: Embracing challenges as opportunities for growth

Disadvantaged students often arrive with fragile confidence and a history of academic setbacks. When tasks are too easy, they learn nothing new; when they're too hard, students disengage. The sweet spot – 'desirable difficulties' (Bjork & Bjork, 2011) – sits in between: challenges that stretch thinking without breaking confidence.

This connects directly to Dweck's (2006) growth mindset research. When students understand that struggle is part of learning – not evidence of failure – they develop resilience and persistence. For disadvantaged learners, this reframing is powerful. It positions them as capable of growth rather than defined by past outcomes.

What it looks like in practice

- Setting tasks just beyond current ability with scaffolding to support
- Celebrating effort and strategy use, not just correct answers
- Using mistakes as learning opportunities through whole-class discussion
- Gradually increasing task difficulty as confidence builds.

Classroom snapshot

A maths teacher introduced 'FAIL = First Attempt In Learning' posters and celebrated productive struggle. When students got stuck, she modelled think-aloud problem-solving rather than jumping to answers. Over time, students began using phrases like *'I haven't figured this out yet'* rather than *'I can't do this'*. Their willingness to tackle harder problems increased significantly.

Strategy 4: Scaffolding with gradual release of responsibility

Scaffolding means providing temporary support that's gradually removed as students develop competence and confidence. The goal isn't to make tasks easier – it's to make success possible while building independence. For disadvantaged students who may have experienced repeated failure, scaffolding provides a pathway to achievement that rebuilds both skill and self-belief.

What it looks like in practice

Scaffolding strategies could include:

- graphic organisers that structure thinking (e.g. planning frames, cause-and-effect diagrams)
- sentence stems for reluctant writers: *'The evidence suggests that... because...'*
- worked examples followed by increasingly independent practice
- think-pair-share activities that let students rehearse ideas before sharing publicly
- checklists and success criteria that make expectations visible.

The scaffold should fade. Start with explicit support, then gradually reduce it as students internalise the strategy. By the end of a unit, students should be able to apply the approach independently.

Strategy 5: Building reflection and using feedback effectively

Reflection isn't just about looking back – it's about learning forward. When students reflect on what worked, what didn't, and why, they develop metacognitive awareness and strategic flexibility. This is particularly important for disadvantaged learners who may not have adults at home helping them process and learn from setbacks.

What it looks like in practice

- Using exit tickets, such as *'What strategy helped you most today?'* and *'What will you try differently next time?'*.
- Learning logs where students can track their progress and strategy use.
- Implementing two stars and a wish: peer feedback that's kind, specific and helpful.
- Completing self-assessment against clear success criteria before submitting work.

Implementation guide

Making metacognition explicit isn't about adding more to an already crowded curriculum; it's about teaching what you're teaching in a way that builds thinking skills alongside content knowledge. Here's a practical sequence for embedding these strategies.

Step 1: Build awareness and shared language

Develop your own understanding of metacognition first, then introduce students to the concept using age-appropriate language. Display key terms – plan, monitor, check, evaluate, adjust – and use them consistently. For students with limited language exposure, provide visual prompts and sentence stems.

Step 2: Model metacognitive thinking

Think aloud regularly: *'I'm not sure how to start this problem... Let me reread the question and look for key words.'* Make your invisible thinking visible. Connect your thinking process to students' own experiences to increase accessibility.

Step 3: Introduce a consistent framework

Use a simple metacognitive cycle across lessons and subjects: 'Plan – Do – Review' or 'Plan – Connect – Check – Monitor – Evaluate'. Scaffold each phase with visuals and sentence starters for students who need additional support.

Step 4: Ask metacognitive questions

Replace *'Are you finished?'* with *'What strategy are you using?'*, *'Why did you choose that approach?'*, *'What will you do if that doesn't work?'*, *'What have you learned that you can use next time?'*. These questions scaffold metacognitive dialogue and gradually transfer responsibility to students.

Step 5: Teach strategies explicitly

Don't assume students know how to use learning strategies – teach them explicitly. Show when and why to use rereading, note-making, elaboration or self-testing. Give time for guided practice with feedback. Make strategy banks visible for all learners.

Step 6: Build in regular reflection

Allocate time at the end of lessons for students to reflect on how they learned, not just what they learned. Use journals, exit tickets or paired discussions. For students who find this difficult, provide structured, guided prompts and celebrate small steps.

Step 7: Create a metacognitive culture

Celebrate effort, strategy use and productive struggle – not just correct answers. Encourage peer support where students share strategies and reflect together. Make success visible for all learners through inclusive examples and diverse approaches.

Step 8: Monitor and adjust

Use observations, student reflections and assessments to track metacognitive growth. Identify students needing additional support and adjust your approach accordingly. Pay particular attention to patterns across disadvantaged groups.

Case Study 1: Metacognitive model for children in highly disadvantaged contexts (Frolli et al., 2021)

Context and problem

A study was carried out in a highly disadvantaged socioeconomic context (details not fully specified in the summary), focusing on children who face structural disadvantages that impact their learning. The research question: can a metacognitive teaching model support basic academic skills (reading, writing, arithmetic) in such contexts?

Intervention

Researchers implemented a metacognitive model intervention in classrooms, where students were taught to become aware of and regulate their cognitive processes.

Specific components included:

- **Self-monitoring and regulation training:** Children were taught to reflect on their thinking (e.g. 'am I understanding this?'), to plan (what strategies they might use), to monitor progress, and to evaluate (how well their strategy worked).

- **Didactic sessions:** Teachers explicitly taught metacognitive strategies, modelling metacognitive dialogue (thinking aloud) during problem-solving, reading and writing tasks.

- **Feedback and reinforcement:** Students received feedback on their use of metacognitive strategies; they were encouraged to continually apply and refine these strategies in their everyday learning.

Outcomes

- **Significant gains:** The study found statistically significant improvements in reading, writing and calculation accuracy in the metacognitive intervention group compared to the control.

- **Improved correctness:** Not only did general performance improve, but the correctness of responses (i.e. fewer mistakes) improved more in the metacognitive group than in the comparison group.

- **Enhanced self-perception:** The authors report that students gained a better perception of their academic abilities, implying increased self-efficacy as they became more aware of their thought processes.

Analysis and lessons

- **Why this worked:** Disadvantaged students often lack access to implicit strategy modelling and may not have been taught how to reflect on their own thinking. Making metacognition explicit gives them tools to self-regulate.
- **Power of explicit dialogue:** Modelling 'thinking aloud' helps students internalise self-monitoring strategies more concretely than just telling them to reflect.
- **Implications for equity:** This suggests that metacognition instruction can be a powerful equaliser. By building metacognitive awareness, students from under-resourced backgrounds can significantly improve foundational academic skills.
- **Teacher training:** For such interventions to succeed, teachers need training and support in metacognitive modelling and feedback.

Broader implications and recommendations

From these case studies, some broader insights emerged.

- **Explicit metacognitive instruction is particularly beneficial for disadvantaged students** because they may not already have strong internal self-regulation habits.
- **Sustained reinforcement matters** because one-off lessons are less effective than embedding metacognitive prompts throughout a course or curriculum.
- **A teacher's role is critical** because teachers must model metacognitive thinking, encourage reflection and provide feedback; they need professional development to do this well.
- **Metacognitive equity** is achieved by teaching metacognition explicitly; educators can help close 'metacognitive gaps' that contribute to achievement disparities.

Case Study 2: Early-years primary school intervention in an inner-city school (Atkins & Doherty, 2022)

Context and problem

In an inner-city primary school serving a high proportion of disadvantaged pupils, teachers found that many students lacked the 'language of learning' – they didn't reflect on how they learned, how they monitored difficulties or how to plan their work. Without this metacognitive awareness, students often struggled to regulate their learning, particularly in challenging tasks.

Intervention

The school implemented a structured metacognitive programme over a term, based on professional development for teachers plus in-class practices:

- **Teacher training:** Three days of professional development introduced teachers to metacognitive theory (planning, monitoring, reviewing), and how to embed it in their teaching.

- **'Plan–Monitor–Review' cycle:** Teachers taught this cycle explicitly. Pupils were guided to plan their task (what to do, what resources), monitor how it was going, and then review (what worked, what didn't).

- **Worked examples and think-alouds:** Teachers modelled their own thinking when solving problems – talking through their planning, when they realised something wasn't working, and how they changed their approach.

- **Reflection and regular feedback:** Students were prompted regularly to reflect on their learning (e.g. after tasks or tests) and discuss what strategies helped them self-regulate.

Outcomes

- **Improved metacognitive awareness:** Students showed a clearer understanding of themselves as learners. In interviews, they mentioned checking their answers, choosing strategies and knowing when they found things hard.

- **Increased self-efficacy:** Several students reported greater confidence and persistence: e.g. 'I don't give up easily' and 'I know how to learn things now'.
- **Shared language and agency:** Teachers observed that having a common vocabulary around learning (plan, monitor, review) gave the pupils more control over their work. According to one teacher, 'it levels things' – disadvantaged students gained tools and awareness that some more advantaged peers may have already had.

Analysis and lessons

- **Why it helped:** By making metacognition explicit, disadvantaged students were given strategies and a shared framework to manage their learning – something they might not have internalised otherwise.
- **The role of teacher modelling:** The 'think-aloud' approach was crucial. When teachers externalise their thinking, students see how planning and evaluation work in practice.
- **Sustainability and equity:** The intervention suggests that even relatively simple metacognitive routines can 'level the playing field' by giving students practical tools and confidence.
- **Implications:** Schools with many disadvantaged pupils can benefit from investing in teacher training on metacognitive practices. Supporting structured reflection cycles may yield strong returns in student self-regulation and motivation.

Broader insights from Case Study 1 and Case Study 2

Explicit metacognitive instruction equips disadvantaged learners with strategies they would not otherwise acquire

Both cases show that students facing socioeconomic or structural disadvantage often lack exposure to metacognitive thinking. When strategies such as planning, monitoring, evaluating and self-questioning were taught explicitly, students gained:

- awareness of their own thinking

- strategies for approaching difficult tasks
- a clearer sense of how to learn rather than just what to learn.

This pattern appears in both the primary-school setting (Case Study 2) and the broader disadvantaged context (Case Study 1).

Teacher modelling (thinking aloud) is a central mechanism for developing metacognitive skills

In both studies, teachers modelling their own thought processes was critical:

- In Case Study 1, teachers used metacognitive dialogue during reading, writing and problem-solving.
- In Case Study 2, teachers verbalised their planning, adjustments and checking strategies while solving problems.

This modelling transformed abstract ideas (e.g. monitor your understanding) into observable actions students could imitate. For disadvantaged pupils, who may not encounter such modelling outside school, this direct demonstration was particularly impactful.

Structured metacognitive routines help students regulate learning and tackle difficulties more effectively

Both cases implemented clear, repeatable frameworks:

- Case Study 1 embedded continuous Plan–Monitor–Evaluate routines through strategy training and feedback.
- Case Study 2 used the Plan–Monitor–Review cycle.

These structures gave students predictable steps to follow when approaching tasks. As a result, learners became:

- more systematic in their work
- better at identifying confusion
- more able to adjust strategies rather than stop when stuck.

This regular structure is essential for students who may not have internalised self-regulation habits.

Improvements were observed in both academic performance and accuracy

Case Study 1 showed statistically significant gains in:

- reading
- writing
- calculation accuracy
- reduced mistakes.

Case Study 2 showed improvements in:

- selecting appropriate strategies
- checking work
- knowing when material was difficult.

Together, these suggest that explicit metacognition instruction strengthens fundamental academic processes and reduces error rates – particularly meaningful gains for disadvantaged learners.

Metacognition enhances learners' confidence and sense of agency

Both case studies found that when students understood how to regulate their own learning:

- confidence increased
- self-efficacy improved
- persistence became more common
- students began to view themselves as capable learners.

In Case Study 1, learners formed a more positive perception of their academic abilities. In Case Study 2, pupils articulated greater control ('I know how to learn things now'). Across both contexts, metacognition appears to strengthen motivational and emotional aspects of learning, not just cognitive ones.

Teacher training is essential for effective and equitable implementation

Both studies included explicit teacher development:

- Case Study 1: training in delivering strategy instruction and metacognitive dialogue.
- Case Study 2: multi-day professional development on planning, monitoring and evaluation.

This indicates that metacognitive teaching is a learned practice, not an automatic one. Without teacher preparation:

- metacognitive routines may be inconsistently applied
- modelling may not be explicit enough
- feedback on students' metacognition may be limited.

For disadvantaged contexts, teacher training is therefore a core component of equitable implementation.

Metacognitive instruction functions as an equity lever

Across the two case studies, explicit metacognition helped 'level the playing field' by providing:

- a shared language for learning
- strategies typically acquired informally by more advantaged students
- opportunities to build self-regulation regardless of background.

Both studies show that when metacognition is intentionally taught, disadvantaged learners close gaps, not by being given simpler work but by gaining access to the same learning strategies that advantaged peers often acquire implicitly.

Making metacognition explicit is a necessary component of effective teaching, particularly for those learners who do not have access to academic support beyond the classroom. The strategies outlined in this chapter – retrieval practice, analogies, scaffolding, challenge and reflection – are not isolated techniques. They are part of a coherent approach to developing independent, self-regulated learners who can monitor and direct their own progress.

Conclusion

This is how we close the gap – not through additional interventions or programmes, but through systematic, explicit teaching of the thinking processes that underpin successful learning. In the following chapter, we examine how these principles apply across subject disciplines, and how teachers can adapt metacognitive strategies to meet the specific demands of maths, English, science and beyond. We make these subject-specific strategies explicit, accessible and achievable.

Key takeaways

- Implementation need not be complex. Begin with one strategy and embed it consistently over time. Model your thinking aloud. Ask purposeful questions that prompt reflection and strategic decision-making. Provide scaffolds that support learners in the moment and fade as confidence grows. Create space for students to consider how they learn, not just what they learn.
- Each time you make your thinking visible, you are equipping students with the tools to do the same. Each time you structure a task to promote independence, you are building both competence and confidence. Each time you ask, *'What strategy will you use?'*, you are reinforcing the message that learning is active, deliberate and within their control.

7 Subject-specific metacognitive strategies

By tailoring metacognitive approaches to the unique demands of each subject – such as problem-solving in mathematics, source analysis in history or planning in writing – we can equip learners with the tools they need to think strategically and independently. We will examine how teachers can explicitly model subject-relevant thinking processes, scaffold reflective questioning and build routines that promote self-regulation. With a focus on practical examples and classroom application, this chapter highlights how metacognitive instruction within each subject can narrow the attainment gap and support long-term learner growth.

Research summary: Self-regulated learning

- Study: Zimmerman (2002) – theoretical framework based on extensive research into metacognition and learner autonomy.
- Key finding: Effective learners actively manage their own learning through planning, monitoring and reflection. These metacognitive behaviours build independence and confidence, particularly for pupils with limited external support.
- Practical implication: Teaching self-regulation explicitly helps all pupils become more strategic and resilient. Embedding subject-specific strategies – such as error logs in maths, reciprocal reading in English and concept mapping in science – gives disadvantaged learners structured ways to take ownership of their learning.

Subject-specific metacognitive strategies offer disadvantaged students structured and empowering ways to engage with learning. In mathematics, techniques like error logs and self-questioning develop analytical habits. In English, tools such as reciprocal reading and reflective planners nurture comprehension and expression. In science, concept mapping and strategy journals promote deeper understanding and transferable problem-solving skills. These approaches, when scaffolded and embedded into daily practice, enable disadvantaged learners not only to access the curriculum but to take ownership of their educational journey.

Metacognition in English

English demands high levels of comprehension, inference and composition – areas where disadvantaged students may lack the confidence or strategies to succeed. Metacognitive support in English can centre around reading and writing processes.

Subject-specific metacognitive strategies for reading and writing

Metacognition – thinking about one's own thinking – is a powerful tool in the development of reading and writing skills, especially for disadvantaged students. These learners often face barriers such as reduced access to language-rich environments, lower confidence in their academic ability, and underdeveloped self-regulation skills. By embedding subject-specific metacognitive strategies into reading and writing instruction, educators can help disadvantaged students become more reflective, strategic and independent in their learning.

In reading, metacognitive strategies guide students to plan, monitor and evaluate their comprehension.

Quick guide

1   Before reading, students should be encouraged to activate prior knowledge by asking questions such as: *What do I already know about this topic?*

2   During reading, they can engage in self-questioning: *Does this make sense? What is the author trying to say? Should I reread this paragraph?*

3   After reading, evaluative questions help consolidate understanding: *What was the main idea? What have I learned? How does it connect to what I knew before?*

One effective classroom approach is reciprocal reading, where students take turns leading discussions that include predicting, clarifying vocabulary, questioning content and summarising meaning. This technique not only supports comprehension but also builds confidence and dialogue skills, which are often underdeveloped in disadvantaged learners. Graphic organisers, charts or dual-coding strategies can further support students in making their thinking visible and structured.

In writing, metacognitive strategies are crucial at all stages of the writing process. During planning, students benefit from structured prompts: *'What is my purpose for writing?'*, *'Who is my audience?'*, *'What structure should I use?'*. These questions can be supported through visual tools like storyboards, paragraph planners and genre-specific templates.

While writing, students can be encouraged to monitor their progress using questions such as: Does this sentence support my main idea? Is my grammar and punctuation accurate? Have I used the right tone and vocabulary? After writing, self-evaluation checklists can prompt students to assess the effectiveness of their communication: *'Did I meet my writing goal?'*, *'What worked well?'*, *'What can I improve next time?'*. Peer-assessment activities, when scaffolded appropriately, also promote critical thinking and reflective dialogue.

Classroom snapshot: Improving confidence through metacognitive writing scaffolds

At a secondary school in Manchester with a high proportion of disadvantaged students, a Year 7 English teacher introduced a metacognitive writing framework for narrative tasks. Each pupil received a 'Plan–Write–Reflect' scaffold that included sentence starters such as 'I am writing this because…' and 'My audience needs to know…'. As pupils progressed, they completed reflective questions after each task, focusing on what they found challenging and what strategies helped them succeed.

Over one term, the teacher observed notable improvements in the students' confidence and quality of writing. In pupil feedback, several students reported feeling more in control of their learning, saying the prompts 'helped them think clearly' and 'made it easier to improve'. The school's literacy coordinator reported a significant reduction in underdeveloped or off-topic writing in assessments.

Metacognition in mathematics

Mathematics often presents a particular challenge for disadvantaged students, many of whom may struggle with self-efficacy or negative beliefs about their abilities. Metacognitive strategies in maths can help students shift from passive problem-solving to active self-regulation.

In mathematics, metacognitive strategies help students approach problems strategically rather than through guesswork. Disadvantaged students benefit from structured prompts such as: *'What is the question asking?'*, *'What strategy should I use?'*, *'Have I checked my answer?'*. These can be embedded into maths journals or classroom posters. Another effective tool is an error analysis log, where students reflect on mistakes, identify misconceptions and plan how to avoid them in the future. This not only builds resilience but also fosters deeper understanding.

Quick guide

1. Thinking aloud and worked examples

One practical technique is thinking aloud while solving problems. Teachers model their internal dialogue as they approach a problem: *'What is the question asking?'*, *'What information do I already have?'*, *'What strategies have worked for similar problems?'*. Disadvantaged students benefit from explicit modelling that makes the problem-solving process visible and repeatable.

2. Self-questioning frameworks

Encouraging students to use self-questioning prompts – such as *'Do I understand the question?'*, *'Have I checked my answer?'* or *'Is there another way to solve this?'* – helps them monitor and evaluate their work. These prompts can be displayed on maths learning mats or posters for regular use.

3. Error analysis logs

Error analysis teaches students to view mistakes as learning opportunities. After solving a set of problems, students can reflect: *'Where did I go wrong?'*, *'What should I do differently next time?'*. Maintaining an error log supports growth mindset and fosters self-awareness.

Classroom snapshot: Improving problem-solving with metacognitive strategies in a Year 8 maths class

In a Year 8 maths class at a school with a high proportion of disadvantaged students, a teacher introduced the 'Read, Plan, Solve, Check' framework to improve problem-solving skills. Initially, many students struggled with breaking down problems and often made avoidable errors due to lack of planning or self-monitoring. After explicit teaching and regular use of the strategy, students began to use the framework more naturally. One student, previously disengaged with the subject, started asking more reflective questions during lessons. She was able to articulate how she was using estimation to check her work and would often revise her approach mid-task when she recognised errors. Over time, there was a noticeable improvement in both her confidence and her problem-solving accuracy.

The teacher also noted that by encouraging students to self-reflect and evaluate their solutions, students developed a stronger sense of ownership over their learning. The class showed a marked increase in engagement, with many students reporting they felt more in control of their learning and understood the steps they were taking to reach a solution.

Metacognitive strategies help students move from passive to purposeful problem-solving. For disadvantaged learners, who may lack confidence or prior success in maths, these strategies offer a structured way to approach tasks with greater independence and clarity.

In mathematics, metacognition involves four key phases: **planning, connecting, monitoring** and **evaluating**. A simple framework such as *Read, Plan, Solve, Check* can support this process.

- **Planning:** Before starting, students should ask themselves questions like *'What is the problem asking me?'* and *'What do I already know that could help?'*. This encourages a strategic approach rather than guesswork. Teachers can scaffold this phase by modelling how to break down problems, identify knowns and unknowns, and select appropriate methods.

- **Connecting:** During this phase, students can link prior knowledge to the new learning or problem by asking reflective questions such as:

  - What does this problem remind me of? Have I solved something similar before?

- Can I represent this in another way-like a drawing, table, graph, or equation?
- How is this problem similar to or different from ones I've done before?
- What information do I already know that might help here?
- Where have I seen this kind of relationship or pattern before?
- Can I break this into smaller parts that connect to simpler problems I understand?

- **Monitoring:** While working, students benefit from prompts such as *'Am I following the correct steps?'*, and *'Is my answer reasonable?'*. These help them self-correct in real time. For example, estimation can be used to check arithmetic answers, while geometric reasoning can support accuracy in shape-based problems. Teachers can reinforce this phase through worked examples and visible prompts in the classroom.

- **Evaluating:** After solving, students should reflect on their process and outcome. Questions like *'Does my answer make sense in context?'* and *'What strategy worked well?'* encourage deeper thinking and support long-term retention. Teachers can guide this reflection with structured prompts or peer discussion, helping students identify what they'd do differently next time.

Disadvantaged students in particular benefit from explicit modelling and consistent scaffolding of these strategies. Tools such as strategy checklists, error analysis logs and self-questioning frameworks make the thinking process visible and repeatable. These approaches not only improve problem-solving accuracy but also foster a sense of ownership and confidence in learning.

Subject-specific metacognitive strategies for science

Metacognitive strategies are essential for promoting deep understanding and independent thinking in science, a subject that often involves complex concepts and problem-solving. Disadvantaged students, in particular, may lack the background knowledge or study skills necessary to approach scientific concepts critically. By embedding metacognitive strategies into science instruction, educators can help students not only learn scientific facts but also understand the process of science, develop problem-solving skills and build confidence in their ability to learn.

In science, metacognitive strategies help students navigate conceptual and procedural knowledge. In biology, concept mapping allows students to visualise relationships between ideas, encouraging them to ask: *'How does this concept connect to others I've learned?'*. In chemistry, using a hypothesis-evidence-conclusion cycle during practical work prompts students to plan and evaluate their thinking. In physics, strategy journals guide learners to reflect on problem-solving approaches: *'What formula did I choose? And why?'*, *'Did it work?'*, *'What would I do differently?'*. These techniques reinforce the habit of thinking about thinking, which is essential in science inquiry.

Quick guide

Metacognitive strategies can be employed at various stages of learning: before, during and after an experiment or concept exploration.

1 Before engaging with a scientific topic, students should be encouraged to set goals and make predictions. For example, when studying chemical reactions, students might be asked: *'What do I know about reactions between acids and bases?'*, *'What do I predict will happen in this experiment?'*. This type of pre-engagement prompts students to activate prior knowledge and think about what they are about to learn, allowing them to make connections with what they already know.

2 During the exploration of scientific concepts, it is important to encourage students to monitor their understanding and adjust their thinking as they proceed. For instance, while conducting an experiment, students should ask themselves: *'What observations am I making?'*, *'How do these observations match my predictions?'*.

3 Encouraging students to regularly check the accuracy of their observations and hypotheses throughout the experiment builds their ability to think critically about the process and results. Teachers can support this by modelling how to ask evaluative questions, such as: *'What evidence do I have to support this conclusion?'* or *'What might I do differently to test my hypothesis more thoroughly?'*.

4 Experiments often require students to assess their results and evaluate their findings. This stage is vital for reinforcing scientific inquiry. After completing an experiment or investigation, students should reflect on their process and results, asking questions such as: *'Did my results align with my expectations?*

Why or why not?', *'What could have caused the discrepancies?'.* By guiding students to reflect on their mistakes and successes, they learn how to refine their approach and develop better hypotheses in future experiments.

These strategies can help students with more theoretical science learning, such as understanding complex models or systems. In subjects like biology or physics, students can ask themselves questions while studying models or diagrams: *'How does this part of the system work?'*, *'What real-life example can I connect this to?'.* These types of questions help students engage more deeply with abstract concepts by relating them to real-world phenomena and encouraging higher-order thinking.

Classroom snapshot: Improving problem-solving in a Year 9 science class

At a secondary school in London, a Year 9 science teacher incorporated metacognitive strategies into her lessons on the concept of energy transfer. Many of her students, particularly those from disadvantaged backgrounds, struggled to grasp the practical applications of energy conservation and transformation. The teacher implemented a strategy that involved pre-lesson predictions, where students were asked to predict how energy would transfer in various scenarios, such as a bouncing ball or a boiling kettle. During the lesson, students monitored their understanding by asking themselves: *'Do I understand how energy moves in this example?',* *'What factors might change the energy transfer in this situation?'.* After the practical demonstrations, students reflected on their observations and compared them to their predictions, discussing any discrepancies.

The teacher noticed that by actively engaging with metacognitive prompts, students not only understood the scientific concepts better but also became more confident in applying these ideas in unfamiliar contexts. One student, who had previously struggled with abstract concepts, was able to explain energy transfer in a new scenario by using the same reasoning processes learned from the reflective questions in class. This deeper understanding of how to approach scientific problems transferred into improved performance in assessments and increased student engagement.

The classroom snapshot of a Year 9 science class illustrates the power of metacognitive strategies in helping students develop the skills needed for independent scientific thinking, especially for disadvantaged learners who may lack the background knowledge and support to navigate complex concepts alone.

Subject-specific metacognitive strategies for history

Metacognitive strategies in history are essential for helping students develop critical thinking, interpret primary sources and analyse historical events. Disadvantaged students, who may not have access to the same historical contexts or vocabulary as their peers, can greatly benefit from metacognitive practices that guide them through the process of thinking about history – examining not just what happened, but why it happened and how we know about it. By using metacognitive strategies, students become more self-aware of their thinking, enabling them to approach history with deeper understanding and critical reflection.

Quick guide

Metacognitive strategies can be employed at each stage of the historical inquiry process: before, during and after studying a historical topic.

1   Before exploring a new topic, students can engage in prediction and inquiry by asking themselves: *'What do I already know about this topic?'*, *'What questions do I have?'*, *'What do I want to learn?'*. These questions help activate prior knowledge and set a clear purpose for learning. For example, when studying the causes of World War I, students can reflect on prior knowledge about Europe's political climate, alliances and tensions, preparing them to engage more meaningfully with the material.

2   During the study of historical events, students should regularly monitor their understanding. For example, when analysing a primary source document such as a letter or speech, students can ask: *'What is the author's perspective?'*, *'How does this source contribute to my understanding of the event?'*, *'What assumptions is the author making?'*. This kind of questioning helps students move beyond surface-level reading and engage critically with sources. Teachers can model how to ask these questions and guide students in breaking down complex sources to recognise bias, perspective and context.

3 Evaluating historical arguments is a crucial metacognitive skill. After students have engaged with a topic or source, they should be encouraged to reflect on the conclusions they have drawn and assess the evidence that supports them. For example, students might ask: *'How strong is the evidence for this argument?'*, *'Could other interpretations be valid?'*, *'What sources could challenge this view?'*. This reflective practice helps students understand that historical knowledge is often constructed from varying perspectives and sources, while in addition it encourages them to consider alternative viewpoints. Encouraging students to evaluate the credibility and reliability of sources is also key in helping them understand the historiographical process.

In writing history, students should use metacognitive strategies to guide their planning, monitoring and revision. When writing essays or historical analyses, they can begin by asking: *'What is my thesis or central argument?'*, *'What evidence will I need to support my point?'*. During writing, students should regularly check their progress by asking: *'Does this paragraph support my argument?'*, *'Have I integrated evidence effectively?'*. After completing the essay, students can reflect on their work by asking: *'What worked well in my argument?'*, *'What areas need improvement?'*. This process of revision helps students refine their thinking and enhance the clarity of their historical analysis.

Classroom snapshot: Year 10 history class – analysing the causes of World War II

In a Year 10 history class at a school in Manchester with a high proportion of disadvantaged students, the teacher implemented metacognitive strategies to help students analyse the complex causes of World War II. Before studying the topic, students were asked to write down what they already knew about the war and what questions they had about its origins. This pre-lesson reflection helped activate prior knowledge and frame their learning goals.

During the lessons, students were given primary sources such as speeches by Adolf Hitler and British government documents. The teacher modelled how to ask critical questions about these sources, such as: 'What is the author's intention?' and 'What biases might be present in this document?'. After engaging with the sources, students were asked to evaluate the different causes of the war and reflect on the evidence. One student, who had initially struggled with analysing sources, was able to use the metacognitive strategies to identify the differing perspectives between the documents and develop a more nuanced understanding of the war's causes.

The students' essays demonstrated significant improvement as they integrated multiple sources and viewpoints, while using reflective practices to strengthen their arguments. The teacher reported that students were more engaged and confident in their ability to critically assess historical events.

The classroom snapshot of the Year 10 history class highlights how metacognitive strategies can help students approach history with a critical mindset, engage deeply with sources and build their skills in historical analysis.

Subject-specific metacognitive strategies for geography

Metacognitive strategies in geography are vital for developing students' understanding of spatial relationships, environmental processes and the interconnection between human and physical geography. Disadvantaged students often face challenges in connecting theoretical knowledge to real-world applications. Metacognitive strategies can help bridge this gap by fostering critical thinking, self-regulation and reflective practices. By teaching students to think about how they approach geographical questions, educators can empower them to become more independent learners, better problem-solvers and critical evaluators of geographical information.

Quick guide

In geography, metacognitive strategies can be applied at various stages of the learning process, from gathering data and making predictions to analysing results and reflecting on conclusions.

1 One key strategy is goal setting before beginning a topic or study of a geographical issue. For example, when studying urbanisation, students can be asked: *'What do I already know about urbanisation?'*, *'What are the key issues surrounding this topic?'*, *'What do I want to find out?'*. This encourages students to identify gaps in their knowledge and establish clear objectives for learning, helping them engage with the material more meaningfully.

2   During the exploration of a geographical topic, students should regularly monitor their understanding and adjust their thinking. For example, when studying population growth or climate change, students can be prompted with questions like: *'Does this data align with what I expected?'*, *'What patterns am I observing?'* or *'How do I interpret these statistics in the context of geographical theories?'*. This helps students critically evaluate the information they are encountering and make connections between concepts. Encouraging them to pause and reflect during lessons or fieldwork provides opportunities for them to assess their progress and ensure they are developing a deeper understanding of the topic.

3   Evaluation of geographical data and sources is a crucial skill that can be developed through metacognitive strategies. After collecting data, students can reflect on how the data supports or challenges their hypotheses. Questions such as *'What are the limitations of this data?'* or *'What assumptions have I made about the sources?'* help students evaluate the credibility and reliability of their sources. In studying physical geography, for instance, when analysing maps or weather patterns, students should reflect on how well the data represents real-world conditions and what factors may influence accuracy.

In project-based assessments, students can benefit from reflecting on their planning, execution and final product. For instance, when writing an essay on climate change impacts, students can use metacognitive strategies like: *'What argument am I trying to make?'*, *'What evidence do I need to support my argument?'*. During writing, students can monitor their work by checking if their evidence logically supports their conclusions. After completing their work, they can engage in self-reflection, asking: *'What worked well in my analysis?'*, *'What could I improve in my reasoning or use of sources?'*.

Classroom snapshot: Year 11 geography class – investigating urbanisation in a local area

In a Year 11 geography class at a school in a low-income area, the teacher introduced metacognitive strategies while studying urbanisation and its effects on local communities. The teacher encouraged students to engage in pre-lesson reflection by asking: 'What do we already know about urbanisation?' and 'What do we want to find out about how urbanisation has affected our local area?'. Students were then tasked with collecting data from local surveys, maps and interviews with residents.

During the investigation, students were prompted to monitor their understanding by asking questions like: What trends are we seeing in the data? How do these trends relate to what we have learned about urbanisation in class? After collecting the data, the teacher guided students in evaluating their sources by asking: 'Is the data reliable?', 'How can we ensure our findings are accurate?'. In writing their final report, students used reflective prompts such as: 'How well did I explain the impact of urbanisation on local infrastructure?' and 'What evidence did I overlook or under-analyse?'.

The use of metacognitive strategies not only improved students' understanding of urbanisation but also enhanced their critical thinking skills. The teacher observed a marked improvement in students' ability to evaluate sources, analyse data and connect their findings to broader geographical theories. One student, previously disengaged with the subject, was able to write a well-reasoned report by using reflective questions throughout the data collection and analysis process.

The classroom snapshot of a Year 11 geography class demonstrates how metacognitive strategies can help students engage with geographical topics in a meaningful way, improving both their understanding of the content and their ability to reflect critically on the knowledge they acquire.

Metacognitive and cognitive scaffolding and differentiation for disadvantaged learners

Metacognitive and cognitive scaffolding are vital strategies in supporting disadvantaged learners, who often face barriers such as limited prior knowledge, reduced access to learning support outside of school, and lower confidence in their academic abilities. These strategies offer structured support that promotes independence, critical thinking and self-regulation by helping students understand how to learn, not just what to learn. When integrated with thoughtful differentiation, scaffolding ensures that every learner receives the right level of challenge and support, tailored to their individual starting points.

Cognitive scaffolding refers to the structured support that helps students understand content by breaking tasks into manageable parts and guiding their thinking. This can include worked examples, sentence starters, visual organisers, cue cards and modelling. For instance, in a science lesson, a teacher might scaffold the process of designing an experiment by providing a template that guides students through each stage: hypothesis, variables, method and conclusion. By modelling the process step-by-step, students develop a cognitive framework they can later apply independently.

Metacognitive scaffolding goes a step further by helping students reflect on their thinking and learning processes. It involves teaching students to plan, monitor and evaluate their learning. Teachers can do this through prompts such as: *'What strategy will I use to solve this problem?'*, *'How do I know this answer makes sense?'*, *'What could I do differently next time?'*. These reflective questions, when embedded in everyday practice, enable students to become more self-aware and strategic learners.

For disadvantaged learners, who may not have had consistent exposure to such learning behaviours, combining metacognitive and cognitive scaffolding with differentiation is particularly effective. Differentiation involves adapting content, process or outcome to meet diverse needs. For example, one student might need a simplified version of a text with vocabulary support, while another benefits from enrichment tasks that extend learning. Scaffolded tasks allow students to access the same objectives through different routes, ensuring high expectations are maintained for all.

Classroom snapshot: Year 6 mixed-ability English session

At a primary school with a high proportion of disadvantaged pupils, a Year 6 teacher implemented a structured writing unit on persuasive texts using both cognitive and metacognitive scaffolding. The class included students with low reading ages, limited vocabulary and low confidence in writing. The teacher began by modelling a persuasive letter using a 'think aloud' strategy, demonstrating not only how to construct arguments but also how to monitor tone, audience and effectiveness.

Next, pupils used sentence stems, vocabulary banks and planning templates to build their own letters. Throughout the process, they were prompted to use metacognitive self-questioning, such as: 'Have I included enough evidence to persuade my reader?', 'How well does my conclusion summarise my argument?'. Less confident students received additional prompts and checklists, while more fluent writers were encouraged to self-assess using peer review protocols. The outcomes showed marked improvement in writing structure, vocabulary use and overall clarity, particularly among disadvantaged students who had previously struggled.

The teacher noted that regular reflection helped pupils internalise the steps of writing and develop ownership over their learning.

The classroom snapshot of the Year 6 English session demonstrates how scaffolding and differentiation can empower disadvantaged learners by building both their cognitive skills and metacognitive awareness.

Taking ownership over learning

Metacognitive strategies play a crucial role in helping students take ownership of their learning. These strategies – planning, monitoring and evaluating one's own thinking – equip learners with tools to become independent, reflective and self-regulated. For disadvantaged students in particular, metacognitive instruction helps bridge gaps in background knowledge, builds confidence and provides a clear structure for engaging with learning tasks. By explicitly teaching metacognition, educators shift the focus from passive reception of information to active, empowered learning.

Ownership of learning occurs when students feel responsible for their progress and understand the steps they can take to improve. Teaching metacognitive strategies fosters this sense of agency by making learning visible. For example, when students are taught to set goals at the beginning of a task, monitor their progress during learning and evaluate the effectiveness of their strategies afterward, they start to see learning as a process they can control. This contrasts with learners who feel that success is based purely on natural ability or external factors, which often leads to disengagement – especially among those who have experienced failure.

A key part of metacognitive development involves modelling. Teachers can demonstrate their own thinking processes out loud, explaining how they tackle a problem, deal with confusion or revise their strategy. Over time, students internalise these processes and begin to apply them independently. Prompt questions like *'What do I already know?'*, *'What's my strategy?'* and *'What will I do differently next time?'* encourage students to reflect on their learning before, during and after tasks. This reflection builds self-awareness, helping students to identify what works best for them, which is fundamental to ownership.

For disadvantaged students, this is especially transformative. Many have not developed academic resilience or strategic learning habits at home. Metacognitive instruction fills this gap by providing tools to cope with setbacks, reflect on effort and adjust strategies. It supports not only academic progress but emotional growth, as students become more confident and capable of managing their learning journey.

Metacognitive moment: Year 7 maths class – building ownership through metacognitive strategy use

In a secondary school with a high proportion of disadvantaged students, a Year 7 maths teacher introduced metacognitive strategies to improve problem-solving. Many students in the class were underachieving and displayed low confidence in maths. The teacher began each lesson by setting clear learning objectives and asking students to plan how they would approach the task, using prompts like *'What strategy might I try?'* and *'What steps will I take?'*.

During problem-solving tasks, students were encouraged to pause and reflect using checklists: *'Does my method make sense?'*, *'Is there another way to solve this?'*. After tasks, they used reflection journals to evaluate their performance: *'What worked well?'*, *'What was difficult?'*, *'What would I do differently next time?'*. Initially scaffolded by the teacher, these reflections gradually became more student-led.

After a term, the teacher observed increased engagement and a noticeable shift in students' attitudes. One student who had previously been reluctant to participate began articulating their strategies aloud and supporting peers in group work. Test scores improved, but more significantly, students spoke with increased ownership over their progress, saying, *'I know how to fix it if I get it wrong'* and *'I figured out what strategy works best for me'*.

Implementation guide for SLT

Implementing subject-specific metacognitive strategies

✓ Promote awareness of metacognition and its benefits for disadvantaged students among staff.

✓ Provide targeted professional development focused on subject-specific metacognitive techniques.

✓ Encourage departments to identify key thinking processes within their subjects.

✓ Support teachers in modelling and embedding metacognitive strategies in lessons.

✓ Facilitate collaboration for sharing best practices and resources across subjects.

✓ Monitor the implementation and impact of these strategies through observations and data.

✓ Allocate time and resources for ongoing training and reflection.

✓ Celebrate successes and continuously refine approaches to maximise student growth.

Next steps

- Identify key thinking skills specific to your subject.
- Model these metacognitive strategies explicitly during lessons.
- Use subject-focused prompts and questions to guide student reflection.
- Incorporate regular opportunities for students to plan, monitor and evaluate their work.
- Provide scaffolds such as graphic organisers, checklists or sentence starters tailored to your subject.
- Gradually release responsibility to encourage independent metacognitive practice.
- Differentiate support to meet the needs of disadvantaged pupils.
- Reflect on and adjust strategies based on student progress and feedback.

Key Takeaways

- Subject-specific metacognitive strategies offer powerful opportunities to support disadvantaged students in becoming more confident, independent learners.
- By embedding tailored approaches into each subject, educators can help students navigate complex tasks, reflect on their thinking and make informed decisions about their learning.
- These strategies not only improve academic outcomes but also foster resilience and self-belief.
- When metacognitive thinking is explicitly modelled and consistently practised across the curriculum, disadvantaged pupils are better equipped to overcome barriers and thrive.
- By making thinking visible in every subject, we create inclusive classrooms where all learners can access success and develop essential lifelong learning skills.

The next chapter focuses on monitoring student progress through practical tools and tracking methods. It highlights how teachers can use checklists, reflection logs and digital platforms to capture metacognitive growth, helping disadvantaged students visualise their learning journey, identify challenges early and celebrate achievements to boost motivation and self-regulation.

.

8 Monitoring progress in metacognitive growth

Research summary: Metacognition and cognitive monitoring

- Study: Flavell (1979) Metacognition and cognitive monitoring – new area of cognitive–developmental inquiry.
- Methodology: Rather than presenting new experiments, Flavell reviewed existing research to show why metacognition is important. He explained the difference between cognitive processes – actually performing tasks like reading or calculating – and metacognitive processes, which involve being aware of and regulating your thinking while completing those tasks. By understanding this distinction, teachers can better support students in becoming reflective, independent learners who monitor and adjust their own thinking as they work.
- Key findings: Flavell distinguished between cognitive processes (such as reading or calculating) and metacognitive processes, which involve monitoring and controlling those tasks. He identified two key components: *metacognitive knowledge* and *metacognitive regulation*. Metacognitive knowledge includes understanding one's own strengths and weaknesses (person knowledge), recognising the demands of a task (task knowledge), and knowing which strategies are most effective (strategy knowledge). Metacognitive regulation refers to the active process of checking, adjusting and guiding one's thinking while working.
- Practical implications: Flavell's work laid the foundation for teaching learners to become more reflective and independent. By helping students understand how they think – and how to manage that thinking – educators can support deeper learning, better problem-solving and the development of self-regulated learners.

Flavell's contribution to metacognitive theory

Flavell (1979) was the first to define metacognition as the awareness and regulation of one's own thinking. His work laid the foundation for understanding how learners plan, monitor and evaluate their cognitive efforts. In this seminal paper, Flavell emphasised the importance of cognitive monitoring – the process of overseeing one's own mental activity during learning. He explored how learners track their comprehension, memory and progress, and how they make decisions based on this internal feedback.

Crucially, Flavell noted that this ability develops over time and is shaped by experience and instruction. Young children often lack the metacognitive awareness needed to recognise when they're struggling or to adjust their approach. As learners mature, their capacity to reflect on and regulate their thinking increases, though this trajectory is highly individual.

Flavell's insights continue to inform classroom practice. By teaching students to monitor their thinking, educators can help them become more accurate in judging their understanding, more strategic in their approach and more resilient when faced with challenge. This is particularly important for disadvantaged learners, who may not have had consistent opportunities to develop these skills. When metacognitive strategies are taught explicitly and embedded into everyday learning, they support not just academic success but long-term independence.

The importance of monitoring metacognitive growth

Metacognition is a critical component of successful learning. It encompasses a range of skills such as planning, monitoring and evaluating learning strategies. While teaching metacognitive strategies is important, monitoring their development over time is equally essential. Regular and thoughtful monitoring allows educators to support learners in becoming more independent, self-aware and capable of directing their own learning. This process is especially beneficial for disadvantaged students who may not have developed metacognitive habits informally or who lack the support structures to reflect on their learning outside the classroom.

Monitoring metacognitive growth enables teachers to understand how students approach learning tasks. Unlike traditional assessments that focus solely on outcomes (e.g. correct answers or grades), monitoring metacognition sheds light on the *processes* students use. It provides insights into whether students are setting goals, selecting strategies, checking their understanding and adapting when things don't go as planned. For instance, if a student consistently fails to review their work or recognise errors, this signals a need for targeted support in self-monitoring rather than content knowledge alone.

According to Flavell (1979), metacognition involves both knowledge about cognition and the regulation of cognitive processes. Monitoring helps educators assess both dimensions: what students know about how they learn, and how well they apply this understanding in real contexts. Without consistent monitoring, teachers may overlook subtle but significant shifts in a learner's capacity to self-regulate, such as when a student begins to use helpful strategies without being prompted, or when they articulate their thinking during a complex task.

Another important reason for monitoring metacognitive growth is that it promotes a culture of reflection and self-improvement. When students regularly engage in metacognitive reflection, through journals, checklists, discussions or digital tools, they start to develop a stronger sense of ownership over their learning. They learn to ask themselves *'What worked?'*, *'What didn't?'* and *'What could I try next time?'*. Over time, these habits foster greater independence, confidence and resilience – qualities that are particularly transformative for students who may struggle with self-belief or past academic setbacks.

Monitoring also allows educators to adapt instruction and provide targeted scaffolding. If students are not progressing in metacognitive skills, it may indicate that the strategies being taught are too abstract or not sufficiently modelled. In contrast, visible progress – such as improved use of planning strategies or greater reflection in journals – can affirm that teaching approaches are effective and should be continued or expanded. It also gives teachers the opportunity to celebrate progress, reinforcing the idea that how students learn is just as important as what they learn.

Monitoring metacognitive growth is a vital aspect of teaching and learning. It helps educators identify needs, celebrate achievements and provide personalised support. More importantly, it empowers learners to take control of their thinking, fostering lifelong skills that extend far beyond the classroom. For all students – and particularly those facing disadvantage – it is a key driver of meaningful, sustained educational success.

Tools for monitoring metacognitive progress

Metacognitive journals and learning logs

Although metacognition should be developed alongside subject knowledge, keeping metacognitive journals and learning logs are powerful tools that support students in developing self-awareness and control over their learning processes. These reflective practices encourage learners to think critically about how they learn, what strategies they use and how they respond to challenges. By writing regularly about their experiences, students begin to internalise metacognitive habits such as planning, monitoring and evaluating.

A metacognitive journal typically includes prompts that guide students to reflect on specific aspects of their learning. Questions such as *'What strategy did I use today?'*, *'What did I find difficult and how did I respond?'* or *'What will I do differently next time?'* help students make sense of their learning journey. Learning logs may take more structured formats, tracking goals, strategies used, outcomes and reflections on what worked or didn't. These tools can be adapted for different ages and abilities – using sentence starters, visuals or audio recordings to ensure accessibility.

For disadvantaged students, metacognitive journals and logs are especially valuable. They provide a private, consistent space to process learning, develop agency and gain confidence in their ability to grow. They also offer educators insight into students' thinking patterns and allow for targeted feedback and support. When used consistently, these tools shift the focus from performance to process, helping all learners – regardless of background – develop the reflective habits needed for long-term success.

In essence, metacognitive journals and learning logs cultivate thoughtful, self-regulated learners who are better equipped to navigate academic and personal challenges.

Adaptation guidelines

For students with literacy challenges, provide sentence starters, visual prompts or offer options to respond orally using recording tools or apps like Seesaw.

Learning ladders and metacognitive progress maps

Learning ladders and metacognitive progress maps are visual tools that support the development and monitoring of metacognitive skills by breaking them down into incremental, achievable steps. These tools help students understand not only what they are learning, but *how* they are learning – fostering awareness of their cognitive and emotional processes during tasks. When used consistently, they can guide learners in self-assessing their progress, identifying areas for growth and setting personal goals.

A learning ladder typically presents a linear progression of metacognitive behaviours, such as *'I can ask for help when I'm stuck'* or *'I can choose the best strategy for the task'*. These statements move from foundational to more advanced levels of self-regulation. Similarly, metacognitive progress maps provide a broader, often non-linear view, illustrating connections between skills such as planning, monitoring and evaluating across subjects or tasks. These visual tools can be adapted for younger students, English language learners or those with additional needs by incorporating symbols, simplified language or colour coding.

For disadvantaged learners, these tools make the invisible processes of learning explicit. They reduce cognitive load by breaking complex behaviours into manageable parts and provide a sense of direction, which is crucial for building motivation and resilience.

Research by Zimmerman (2002) supports the use of structured self-regulatory tools, noting that self-awareness and strategic action are essential for academic success. Learning ladders and progress maps embody this approach, helping students take ownership of their metacognitive development.

Adaptation guidelines

Create differentiated ladders for various stages of development and use colour-coding or symbols to support learners with processing difficulties. Involve students in designing the ladder to increase ownership.

Self-assessment rubrics and checklists

Rubrics that explicitly outline metacognitive behaviours help students self-assess their progress. For example, a rubric for goal-setting might include statements like:

- 'I do not usually set goals.'
- 'I set goals with support.'
- 'I set goals independently and track them.'

Adaptation guidelines

Keep language clear and simple. Use icons or emoji faces to represent different levels of understanding for younger or EAL students. Allow students to co-construct rubrics where possible.

Exit tickets and metacognitive prompts

Exit tickets and metacognitive prompts are simple yet powerful tools that encourage students to reflect on their learning at the end of a lesson. These strategies help make thinking visible by prompting learners to consider what they learned, how they approached the task, and what strategies they used or could improve. Regular use of these tools builds metacognitive awareness and reinforces the habit of reflection, which is critical for developing self-regulated learners.

An exit ticket might ask questions such as: *'What did I find challenging today and how did I overcome it?'* or *'What strategy worked well for me?'*. These brief responses give students the opportunity to consolidate their learning and articulate their thinking processes. In turn, teachers gain immediate insight into how students are engaging with their learning and which areas may need further support. Metacognitive prompts can be used orally or in writing, either individually or in groups, and tailored for different ages and learning needs.

For disadvantaged students, who may have limited opportunities for guided reflection at home, exit tickets and prompts provide consistent scaffolding to develop critical self-awareness. They also reinforce the message that learning is a process, not just an outcome, which supports resilience and persistence.

According to Schraw and Dennison (1994), fostering metacognitive awareness involves both knowledge about cognition and regulation of cognition. Exit tickets and prompts directly support both components, helping students understand their learning and take steps to improve it.

Adaptation guidelines

Offer choice in format – written, visual or verbal – and have a limit of one or two questions to avoid overwhelming students who may experience cognitive overload.

Learning conferences and reflective conversations

Learning conferences and reflective conversations are structured dialogues between teachers and students that focus on understanding how learning happens, not just what has been learned. These conversations provide a rich opportunity to explore students' thinking processes, decision-making strategies and emotional responses to challenges. By engaging in these discussions, students develop metacognitive awareness and are encouraged to take greater ownership of their learning.

Unlike traditional feedback, learning conferences focus on *process over product*. Teachers might ask: *'What strategies did you try when you got stuck?'* or *'How did you decide which information was most important?'*. Such questions prompt students to analyse their own thinking and articulate their reasoning. These conversations can be embedded into weekly routines or scheduled after major tasks, offering both formative feedback and a moment for self-evaluation.

For disadvantaged learners, reflective conversations are especially powerful. They provide personalised support, build trusting relationships and create space for students to express learning-related anxieties or misconceptions. They also promote a growth mindset, helping students view struggle as part of the learning journey.

A metacognitive moment might occur during a learning conference when a student says, 'At first I rushed, but when I stopped and reread the question, I realised I needed to plan. Next time, I'll slow down earlier.' This awareness signifies a shift from reactive to strategic learning.

Research by McGuinness (1999) supports this approach, emphasising that talking about thinking helps pupils become more independent and metacognitively aware.

Adaptation guidelines

Use sentence stems such as *'Tell me how you decided what to do when...'* to support reluctant speakers. Visual aids or mind maps can be helpful scaffolds for these dialogues.

Digital portfolios and reflection tools

Digital portfolios and reflection tools are increasingly popular methods for fostering metacognitive growth in learners by providing dynamic spaces to collect, review and reflect on their work over time. These digital platforms enable students to document their learning journey, capture evidence of progress and articulate their thinking and decision-making processes. Unlike traditional paper-based methods, digital portfolios offer multimedia capabilities – such as videos, audio recordings and hyperlinks – that cater to diverse learning styles and make reflection more engaging.

Reflection tools embedded within digital portfolios prompt students to regularly analyse what strategies worked, what challenges they encountered, and how they might adjust their approach moving forward. This ongoing process of self-assessment helps students develop deeper metacognitive awareness and encourages ownership of their learning.

For disadvantaged students, digital portfolios can be especially empowering. They provide a safe, organised environment where learners can revisit past work and reflections, track growth at their own pace, and communicate progress with teachers and families. This visibility often boosts motivation and confidence, as students recognise the value of their effort and strategic thinking.

A metacognitive moment can occur when a student uploads a draft and writes, 'I realised I kept making the same mistake in my writing because I wasn't checking my punctuation carefully. Next time, I'll use a checklist before submitting.' This insight demonstrates active reflection and a plan for improvement.

Research by Barrett (2007) highlights that digital portfolios foster self-regulation and metacognitive skills by making learning visible and reflective practices routine.

Adaptation guidelines

Incorporate multimedia options to give all learners a way to demonstrate their thinking. Use templates or structure to support learners who may need help organising their reflections.

Peer feedback and collaborative reflection

Peer feedback and collaborative reflection are vital strategies that promote metacognitive development by encouraging learners to articulate their thinking, evaluate others' work and consider alternative perspectives. When students engage in these processes, they move beyond passive reception of knowledge to active construction and regulation of their learning. This social interaction fosters deeper awareness of cognitive strategies and emotional responses, as well as critical self-assessment skills.

Through peer feedback, students learn to identify strengths and areas for improvement in their classmates' work, which often helps them reflect on their own approaches. Collaborative reflection, whether in pairs or small groups, allows learners to discuss their thought processes, challenges and solutions openly. This dialogue encourages metacognitive questioning, such as *'Why did you choose that method?'* or *'How did you decide to change your strategy?'*.

For disadvantaged learners, peer feedback and collaborative reflection can be particularly empowering. These practices create supportive learning communities where students feel heard and valued. They also provide opportunities to model and scaffold metacognitive strategies in a less formal, lower-stakes environment than teacher-led assessment alone.

A metacognitive moment might arise during a peer review when a student says, *'I thought my approach was fine, but hearing how you planned your steps made me realise I need to be more organised. I'll try your strategy next time.'* This insight reflects increased self-awareness and a readiness to adjust learning strategies.

Research by Topping (2009) emphasises that peer assessment not only enhances academic performance but also develops critical thinking and self-regulatory skills, essential components of metacognition.

Adaptation guidelines

Model effective feedback using video examples or role play, especially for students who may be unfamiliar with giving or receiving constructive comments. Use mixed ability pairing to encourage learning from others.

Quick guide: Creating a culture of metacognitive growth

1 Monitoring tools for metacognitive growth become truly effective when embedded within a broader classroom culture that consistently values and prioritises metacognition. This culture is cultivated through several interconnected elements.

2 Consistency is key. Metacognitive reflection should be a regular part of daily classroom routines, not an occasional activity. Whether through quick exit tickets, brief journaling or class discussions, making reflection habitual helps students develop the mindset that thinking about their thinking is an essential part of learning.

3 Language plays a critical role. Teachers must use metacognitive vocabulary explicitly and frequently. Terms like 'planning', 'monitoring', 'evaluating' and 'strategy' should become part of everyday classroom dialogue. This shared language empowers students to articulate their thought processes and reinforces the importance of metacognitive skills.

4 Visibility also supports growth. Displaying metacognitive prompts, checklists or strategy posters in physical or digital classroom spaces provides constant reminders and scaffolds for students. This accessibility helps learners, especially those who may struggle to self-initiate reflection, to engage more readily with metacognitive practices.

5 Finally, celebration of metacognitive progress alongside academic achievement is crucial. Recognising effort, strategy use and reflective growth builds motivation and resilience, particularly for disadvantaged students. This emphasis helps bridge gaps in self-belief by reframing challenges as valuable learning opportunities rather than fixed limitations.

By weaving these elements together, educators create a supportive environment where all students feel equipped and encouraged to become self-regulated, reflective learners.

Metacognitive moment: Mason's journey towards persistence and self-regulation

Mason, a Year 6 student, had long struggled with task persistence. When faced with challenging assignments, his immediate reaction was often to give up, feeling overwhelmed and unsure of how to proceed. Recognising this barrier to Mason's learning, his teacher introduced a learning ladder designed specifically to help him reflect on and improve his approach to difficult tasks. The ladder included simple, clear phrases representing different levels of persistence and problem-solving: 'I give up easily', 'I try again with help' and 'I keep trying different ways'.

At the outset, Mason placed himself at the middle rung: 'I try again with help.' This honest self-assessment was a crucial starting point – it demonstrated Mason's awareness of his current learning behaviour and set the stage for growth. Over the next several weeks, Mason's teacher integrated learning logs and structured peer feedback sessions into their routine. These tools were carefully scaffolded to encourage Mason to notice when he became stuck, reflect on what strategies he had attempted, and identify the type of assistance he needed.

A turning point came when Mason began independently recognising moments of struggle during tasks. One day, as he was working through a challenging problem, he paused and said, 'I was going to give up, but I thought about what worked last time.' This simple statement was profound. It showed that Mason had started actively monitoring his learning process, drawing on past experiences, and making a conscious decision to adjust his approach. He was no longer passively reacting to difficulty but engaging in deliberate self-regulation – a core metacognitive skill.

Mason's teacher acknowledged this moment not just as a positive behavioural change but as a metacognitive milestone. It marked the beginning of Mason's journey towards greater independence as a learner. By moving from 'I try again with help' towards 'I keep trying different ways', Mason was developing the ability to orchestrate his own learning, one of the fundamental goals of metacognitive growth.

This metacognitive moment highlights the power of making thinking visible and providing learners with concrete frameworks to reflect on their learning. Mason's progress illustrates how scaffolding, targeted feedback and supportive reflection can transform a student's relationship with challenges – shifting from avoidance and frustration to persistence and strategic problem-solving. It's a reminder that metacognition is not an abstract concept but a practical, teachable skill that can empower learners to become resilient, self-directed thinkers.

Metacognitive moment: Liam's development in history

Liam, a Year 10 student, struggled to critically analyse historical sources, often summarising rather than evaluating reliability or bias. To support self-regulation, his teacher introduced a structured reflection framework prompting questions like: 'What is the author's perspective?', 'What evidence supports their claim?', 'Could there be alternative interpretations?'.

Initially, Liam relied on surface-level observations. Over several weeks, he began setting goals, monitoring his thinking and adjusting strategies. Using guided questioning, source comparison charts and peer discussions, he noticed patterns, evaluated evidence and identified gaps in his understanding.

A turning point occurred when analysing conflicting accounts of a twentieth-century event; he wrote, 'This source emphasises one viewpoint, so I need to compare it with another to form a balanced conclusion.'

By planning, monitoring and reflecting independently, Liam developed self-regulation, strengthened critical thinking and gained confidence. He learned to manage his own learning process, make evidence-based judgements, and approach complex historical material strategically.

Conclusion

Monitoring metacognitive growth is not a one-size-fits-all task; it demands a thoughtful, multi-faceted approach that recognises the diverse needs of learners, especially those facing disadvantages. For these students, metacognitive tools and strategies cannot simply be introduced and assumed to work.

Instead, they must be carefully scaffolded, made accessible and continually adapted to address individual challenges and strengths. When educators implement these mechanisms thoughtfully, the impact goes far beyond tracking academic progress. It builds essential confidence, nurtures independence and cultivates students' capacity to become reflective, resilient learners who take ownership of their educational journeys.

Flavell's definition of metacognition as 'active monitoring and consequent regulation and orchestration' of learning highlights that metacognition is a dynamic process requiring deliberate attention and action. However, for many disadvantaged learners, metacognitive growth is often overlooked or under-supported, contributing to gaps in achievement and self-belief. This is a call to educators, administrators and policymakers: prioritise metacognitive growth as a fundamental pillar of learning and provide the tools and structures necessary to make it visible, manageable and meaningful.

To truly empower students, monitoring tools must be embedded within a classroom culture that values metacognition through consistent routines, explicit language, visible prompts and genuine celebration of metacognitive progress. Tools like reflective journals, learning logs, exit tickets and digital portfolios become powerful when students are guided in their use and see their reflections driving real change in their learning approaches. Peer feedback and learning conferences deepen this process by fostering collaborative reflection and building metacognitive dialogue.

Particularly for disadvantaged learners, scaffolding is essential. This means breaking down metacognitive strategies into manageable steps, offering sentence starters or visual aids, and ensuring regular teacher check-ins that support rather than overwhelm. Accessibility also matters – tools must be flexible to accommodate different languages, learning styles and abilities. When students experience success in these scaffolded steps, they gain confidence not just in their academic skills but in their ability to regulate their own learning and navigate challenges independently.

Moreover, the process of monitoring metacognitive growth fosters resilience. Students learn that setbacks and mistakes are not signs of failure but opportunities to analyse, adjust and improve. This shift in mindset is crucial for disadvantaged learners who may have internalised negative beliefs about their abilities.

The power of metacognitive growth monitoring lies in its potential to transform education from a system where students passively receive knowledge to one where they actively engage with and control their learning. This transformation is especially urgent for those students who face systemic barriers – those who need support in developing the very skills that enable lifelong learning and adaptation.

Therefore, it is imperative that schools adopt a deliberate, inclusive approach to monitoring metacognition. Invest in professional development for teachers to understand and implement metacognitive strategies effectively. Provide resources that are adaptable and accessible. Create classroom environments where reflection is valued as much as achievement. Most importantly, listen to students' voices and experiences, adapting approaches to meet their evolving needs.

By committing to this approach, educators can unlock the full potential of metacognition, making it a catalyst for equity and empowerment in education. Let us ensure that every learner, especially the disadvantaged, has the tools and support to monitor, regulate and orchestrate their own learning journey – turning metacognition into a source of confidence, independence and lifelong success.

Implementation checkpoint: Monitoring metacognitive growth

Use this checklist to evaluate your current monitoring practices:

✓ I regularly observe pupils' metacognitive behaviours during independent work.

✓ I use formative assessment to track metacognitive development, not just content knowledge.

✓ Pupils have opportunities to self-assess their metacognitive strategies.

✓ I provide specific feedback on pupils' use of metacognitive strategies (*'I noticed you paused to check your work – that's strategic monitoring'*).

✓ I keep simple records of pupils' metacognitive progress over time.

✓ Pupils can articulate how their thinking strategies have developed.

✓ I adapt my teaching based on what I observe about pupils' metacognitive development.

✓ I celebrate growth in thinking strategies, not just correct answers.

Choose one area to develop this term. What specific action will you take?

Key takeaways

- Monitoring metacognitive growth requires observation of behaviours, not just assessment of content knowledge.
- Simple tracking tools (thinking journals, reflection prompts, observation checklists) provide valuable formative data.
- Pupils benefit from self-assessment opportunities that make their thinking strategies visible.
- Metacognitive development is gradual – look for small shifts in planning, monitoring and evaluating behaviours.
- For disadvantaged pupils, explicit feedback on metacognitive growth builds self-efficacy.
- Progress monitoring should inform teaching – adapt your approach based on what you observe.
- Celebrate metacognitive progress to reinforce its value.

Reflection prompts

For educators:

- How do I currently track pupils' metacognitive development?
- What evidence do I have that pupils are becoming more strategic in their thinking?
- Do I provide feedback on thinking processes as well as content?
- Which pupils have made the most metacognitive progress this term? What supported their growth?

For school leaders:

- How do we monitor metacognitive development across the school?
- What systems exist for sharing effective monitoring practices?
- Do our assessment systems capture thinking skills as well as content knowledge?
- How do we ensure all staff understand what metacognitive progress looks like?

Next steps

1 Choose one simple monitoring tool (observation checklist, thinking tracker, reflection prompt) and trial it for four weeks.

2 Share examples of pupils' metacognitive progress in a staff meeting – make thinking development visible to colleagues.

3 Provide at least three pupils with specific feedback on their metacognitive strategies this week.

4 Create a simple visual display showing the progression of metacognitive skills so pupils can track their own growth.

5 Review one pupil's work samples from the start and end of term – note evidence of metacognitive development.

9 Teaching metacognition for wellbeing

Wellbeing and academic success are closely linked. Students experiencing stress, low self-confidence or challenging home circumstances often struggle to engage fully with learning (Durlak et al., 2011). Disadvantaged learners face additional barriers, including limited access to educational resources, fewer opportunities for structured support and increased exposure to social or economic stressors (Education Endowment Foundation, 2022). While traditional teaching often emphasises content knowledge, research shows that explicitly teaching students *how to learn* can improve both academic outcomes and emotional resilience (Zimmerman, 2002).

By teaching students to plan, monitor, check, connect and evaluate their learning processes, educators help learners gain control over their cognitive and emotional responses (Mughal, 2021). These strategies enable students to manage setbacks, reduce anxiety and approach challenges strategically, fostering confidence and persistence (Norman et al., 2023).

Metacognitive instruction also encourages a growth mindset, helping students see mistakes as learning opportunities rather than failures (Dweck, 2006). For disadvantaged learners, such strategies are especially transformative, bridging gaps in experience and building skills that may not be nurtured outside school (EEF, 2022).

This chapter explores practical approaches for embedding metacognition into classroom practice to promote wellbeing. Drawing on evidence-based research and classroom examples, it demonstrates how reflection, scaffolding and guided self-regulation can help students develop resilience, self-efficacy and a positive relationship with learning.

Defining wellbeing

Wellbeing is a multidimensional concept encompassing physical, mental, emotional and social dimensions of health. It reflects an individual's ability to cope with life challenges, maintain positive relationships and achieve personal and academic goals (Diener et al., 2018). Wellbeing is not simply the absence of mental health problems; rather it includes positive aspects such as life satisfaction, resilience, self-efficacy and a sense of purpose (Huppert & So, 2013). In educational contexts, student wellbeing is closely linked to engagement, motivation and learning outcomes. Students with higher levels of wellbeing are more likely to concentrate effectively, participate actively in learning, and persevere through challenges (Roffey, 2012).

Wellbeing can be broadly categorised into several interconnected domains:

1 **Emotional wellbeing:** The ability to manage emotions, cope with stress and maintain a positive outlook. Emotional wellbeing contributes to resilience in the face of setbacks (Durlak et al., 2011).

2 **Social wellbeing:** The quality of relationships with peers, teachers and family. Social support has been shown to buffer the effects of stress and is critical for mental health (Friedli, 2009).

3 **Psychological wellbeing:** Self-efficacy, self-esteem, autonomy and purpose in life. Psychological wellbeing underpins the motivation to learn and engage with challenges (Ryff, 1989).

4 **Physical wellbeing:** Health-related factors such as sleep, nutrition and exercise directly impact cognitive performance and emotional stability (World Health Organization, 2013).

Challenges to wellbeing in disadvantaged populations

Not all individuals experience high levels of wellbeing. Certain populations, particularly those experiencing socioeconomic disadvantage, are at elevated risk of lower wellbeing due to a range of interrelated factors. Disadvantaged students often face limited access to educational resources, inadequate housing, food insecurity and unstable home environments. These conditions create chronic stressors that can impact both cognitive and emotional development (Reiss, 2013).

Impact of socioeconomic status on wellbeing

Socioeconomic status is one of the most consistent predictors of wellbeing disparities. Low socioeconomic status is associated with reduced access to extracurricular opportunities, learning materials and safe spaces for study, which limits students' ability to engage fully with learning (Sirin, 2005). The stress associated with financial insecurity can lead to heightened anxiety, depression and emotional dysregulation (Evans & Kim, 2013). Children and adolescents experiencing chronic stress are more likely to exhibit behavioural issues, lower academic achievement and reduced self-esteem (Norman et al., 2023).

Psychosocial stressors and mental health

Disadvantaged students may experience additional psychosocial stressors, including exposure to community violence, parental unemployment or familial instability. These stressors can undermine emotional and social wellbeing, making it difficult for students to focus on learning or develop resilience (Reiss, 2013). Emotional dysregulation can exacerbate academic challenges, creating a cycle in which poor wellbeing leads to lower engagement, which in turn reduces confidence and further harms wellbeing.

Barriers to developing coping and self-regulation skills

Students from disadvantaged backgrounds may have fewer opportunities to develop coping strategies, self-regulation skills or problem-solving techniques outside school. These skills are crucial for managing both academic and personal challenges (Zimmerman, 2002). Without support, students may adopt maladaptive responses to stress, such as avoidance, disengagement or learned helplessness. These behaviours further reduce self-efficacy and limit opportunities for positive learning experiences, perpetuating disadvantage (Durlak et al., 2011).

Educational implications

Research indicates that schools can play a vital role in mitigating the impact of disadvantage on wellbeing. Interventions that teach emotional regulation, resilience and metacognitive strategies can help students gain control over their learning and emotional responses (EEF, 2022). For example, explicitly teaching students to plan, monitor and evaluate their work not only improves academic performance but also fosters self-efficacy and emotional resilience (Flavell, 1979; Mughal, 2021).

The role of metacognition in supporting wellbeing

By helping students reflect on how they learn and cope with challenges, metacognitive strategies provide both cognitive and emotional benefits (Mughal, 2021). When students are taught to pause, assess their understanding and adjust their strategies, they are better equipped to manage stress, maintain focus and approach problems with confidence (Zimmerman, 2002). This process reinforces a growth mindset, encouraging students to view setbacks as learning opportunities rather than indicators of failure (Dweck, 2006).

Long-term consequences of poor wellbeing

Neglecting wellbeing in educational contexts has significant and far-reaching consequences, affecting both immediate learning outcomes and longer-term life trajectories. Students who experience low wellbeing often demonstrate reduced engagement in classroom activities, lower motivation to learn and diminished academic performance. Emotional distress, including anxiety, low self-esteem and feelings of helplessness, can further undermine cognitive functioning and the ability to retain or apply knowledge effectively (Friedli, 2009). Over time, these challenges can create a negative feedback loop, where poor wellbeing leads to academic difficulties, and repeated experiences of struggle reinforce feelings of incompetence and disengagement.

The long-term implications of sustained low wellbeing extend beyond academic outcomes. Research indicates that children and adolescents with poor emotional and social wellbeing are at increased risk of developing mental health problems in adulthood, including depression, anxiety and maladaptive coping mechanisms (Norman et al., 2023; Reiss, 2013). Moreover, limited self-regulation and problem-solving skills, which are closely linked to wellbeing, can restrict career opportunities, reduce resilience in facing life challenges, and hinder the ability to form and maintain positive social relationships. These outcomes are particularly pronounced for disadvantaged students, who may encounter additional stressors such as financial insecurity, unstable housing or limited access to supportive learning environments (Evans & Kim, 2013).

Conversely, interventions that actively promote wellbeing can mitigate these risks and foster positive life outcomes. Embedding strategies that develop self-regulation, metacognition and reflective learning within the curriculum equips students with tools to manage both academic and personal challenges (Flavell, 1979; Zimmerman, 2002). For example, explicitly teaching pupils to plan, monitor and evaluate their learning not only enhances academic performance but also builds resilience, persistence and a sense of agency over their own learning. Students learn to view challenges as opportunities rather than insurmountable obstacles, promoting a growth mindset that supports lifelong learning and emotional stability (Dweck, 2006; Mughal, 2021).

Evidence suggests that wellbeing-focused educational interventions can be particularly transformative for disadvantaged learners. By breaking cycles of stress and disengagement, these strategies help pupils develop confidence, self-efficacy and coping skills that extend beyond the classroom (EEF, 2022). For instance, reflection journals, guided metacognitive prompts and collaborative discussions provide structured opportunities to process emotions, evaluate progress and recognise achievements, thereby reinforcing both academic and emotional resilience. Over time, the integration of wellbeing and metacognitive instruction can improve life trajectories by supporting mental health, social competence and lifelong learning habits.

Ultimately, neglecting wellbeing not only limits immediate academic success but also jeopardises longer-term personal development. By recognising the critical link between wellbeing, self-regulation and learning, educators can implement strategies that prevent these negative outcomes, particularly for disadvantaged students. Fostering wellbeing in schools is therefore not a peripheral concern – it is central to ensuring that all students can achieve their full potential academically, socially and emotionally.

Explicitly teaching metacognition to support learning and wellbeing

Explicitly teaching metacognition offers a dual benefit: it develops students' academic skills while simultaneously enhancing their wellbeing. When students learn how to manage their thinking processes, they gain control over their learning journey, which enhances both competence and confidence (Flavell, 1979; Zimmerman, 2002).

Structured lesson designs are critical for embedding metacognitive practices effectively. Teachers can integrate clear learning objectives, step-by-step guidance, and reflection points within everyday activities. For example, primary school teachers might use visual scaffolds such as 'learning ladders' or 'thinking boxes' to guide pupils through planning, monitoring and evaluating their work. Pupils can be prompted to ask themselves questions such as, *'What do I already know about this topic?'*, *'Am I on the right track?'* and *'What strategy could I try next?'* (Mughal, 2021). Secondary students can apply similar strategies in subject-specific contexts, such as analysing sources in history or evaluating problem-solving methods in mathematics. By explicitly structuring opportunities for reflection, teachers help students develop self-regulation, which is closely linked to emotional resilience and academic persistence (EEF, 2022).

Classroom snapshot: Linking metacognition to emotional regulation (Year 4)

Miss Khan noticed her Year 4 class struggled with frustration during challenging tasks. Many pupils, particularly those from disadvantaged backgrounds, would shut down or act out when confused. She decided to explicitly teach the connection between metacognitive strategies and emotional wellbeing.

She introduced the 'Learning Zone Model': Comfort Zone (too easy, we're not learning), Learning Zone (challenging but manageable with strategies) and Panic Zone (too hard, we're overwhelmed). When pupils felt frustrated, she'd ask: *'Which zone are you in? If you're in the panic zone, what strategy could bring you back to the learning zone?'*

She modelled this herself: *'I'm feeling frustrated with this marking. I'm in the panic zone. What could I do? I could break it into smaller chunks – mark five books, take a break, mark five more. I could ask a colleague for help. I could remind myself that feeling stuck is normal and means I'm learning how to manage this better.'*

Over time, pupils began using this framework independently. When Amara felt overwhelmed during a writing task, she said: *'Miss, I'm in the panic zone. How can I break my work into smaller bits?'* Her metacognitive awareness helped her regulate her emotional response and stay engaged.

Collaborative discussions further reinforce metacognitive learning. When students articulate their thinking to peers, they deepen understanding, normalise struggle and learn alternative approaches to tasks. Reflection journals and guided questioning can provide additional support, allowing pupils to monitor their progress, evaluate strategies and consider how setbacks can inform future learning. For disadvantaged students, these practices not only improve academic outcomes but also provide structured support to manage stress, reduce anxiety and build a sense of agency over their learning (Norman et al., 2023).

Prioritising metacognition alongside wellbeing encourages the development of resilient, self-regulated learners. Students who can monitor and adjust their thinking are better equipped to cope with challenges both inside and outside the classroom. They develop confidence in their abilities, see mistakes as learning opportunities and cultivate problem-solving skills that extend beyond academic tasks (Dweck, 2006; Roffey, 2012). For disadvantaged learners who may lack these skills outside of school, metacognitive instruction is transformative, providing tools to navigate both academic challenges and emotional stressors.

Ultimately, teaching metacognition is a call to action for educators. It is not merely an enhancement to classroom practice but a vital approach to improving learning and wellbeing. By modelling thinking, providing scaffolds, structuring reflection and promoting collaborative discussion, teachers can create an environment where all students, particularly those facing disadvantage, develop the skills, confidence and resilience to succeed academically and emotionally.

Metacognition and wellbeing

Thinking about thinking allows students to become aware of how they learn and to regulate their responses to challenges. For disadvantaged students, who may experience heightened stress or a lack of academic support outside school, metacognitive strategies provide tools to manage frustration, develop self-efficacy and build resilience (EEF, 2022). For example, a student struggling with a challenging maths problem can use self-monitoring to recognise confusion, pause and try a new approach rather than giving up. This process supports emotional regulation by reducing anxiety and fostering a sense of control over learning (Norman et al., 2023).

Strategies for primary school pupils

For disadvantaged primary pupils, explicit metacognitive instruction should be highly structured, scaffolded and integrated into everyday learning. These strategies help pupils not only develop academic skills but also build resilience, confidence and self-regulation, which are critical for wellbeing (Mughal, 2021; Zimmerman, 2002).

Visual scaffolds

Visual tools such as learning ladders, 'thinking hats' and visual checklists help pupils recognise their current understanding, identify next steps and plan strategies. For example, in a Year 3 literacy lesson, children could use a 'planning box' to outline a story's beginning, middle and end. By seeing the structure of their thinking visually, pupils can organise their ideas, monitor progress and adjust their approach if necessary. Visual scaffolds also provide a concrete reference for pupils who may struggle with abstract instructions, making metacognitive processes accessible to all learners.

Guided reflection

Teachers can model their thinking aloud, demonstrating strategies and decision-making processes. In a maths lesson, a teacher might verbalise: *'I'm going to check my addition by counting on my fingers and then using the number line to see if it matches.'* Pupils then replicate this process with support, gradually internalising strategies for independent use. Guided reflection allows pupils to observe metacognitive thinking in action, reinforcing problem-solving, error detection and adaptive reasoning (Flavell, 1979).

Structured journals

Short, daily reflection prompts encourage pupils to monitor effort, strategy use and emotional responses. Questions such as, *'What did I do well today?'* or *'What could I try differently tomorrow?'* help pupils develop habits of self-reflection and metacognitive awareness. Journals provide a private space for students to articulate successes, recognise challenges and track progress over time, which is especially valuable for disadvantaged pupils who may lack supportive learning environments outside school (Durlak et al., 2011).

Classroom snapshot: Reflection journals for wellbeing (Year 9)

Mr Thompson introduced weekly reflection journals in his Year 9 English class. Pupils spent the last 10 minutes of Friday lessons completing three prompts: *'What went well this week?', 'What was challenging?', 'What strategy will I try next week?'.*

Initially, pupils struggled to write meaningful reflections. They'd write *'nothing'* or *'it was fine'.* But Mr Thompson persisted, modelling his own reflections and providing sentence starters: *'I felt proud when...', 'I found it difficult to...', 'Next week I'll try...'.*

After a term, the journals revealed important patterns. Several pupils wrote repeatedly about anxiety during group work. This prompted Mr Thompson to explicitly teach collaborative strategies and provide alternative ways to participate. For disadvantaged pupils who rarely talked about their feelings, the journal became a safe space to process emotions and develop self-awareness.

One pupil wrote: *'I always thought I was just bad at English. But now I see I need to plan more. When I plan, my writing is better. That makes me feel less anxious about writing.'* The metacognitive reflection shifted his self-perception from fixed (*'I'm bad at English'*) to strategic (*'I need to plan more'*).

Collaborative reflection

Small-group discussions allow pupils to share strategies, normalise mistakes and recognise multiple approaches to learning tasks. Collaborative reflection fosters emotional safety, resilience and social wellbeing while supporting the development of problem-solving skills. Pupils learn that errors are part of the learning process, reducing fear of failure and enhancing persistence (Mughal, 2021).

In a Year 4 science lesson on plants, the teacher begins with a planning activity, asking students to predict which plants will grow fastest and why. Throughout the experiment, pupils monitor growth, record observations and check their predictions against results. At the end of the unit, students evaluate their approach and reflect on what they would do differently next time. This structured reflection helps pupils manage frustration when outcomes do not match expectations, reinforcing resilience and a sense of agency.

Strategies for secondary school pupils

Metacognitive strategies for secondary students build on foundational skills developed in primary school, with increased complexity and independence. For disadvantaged learners, these strategies support self-regulation, reduce academic anxiety and strengthen both cognitive and emotional skills (EEF, 2022; Zimmerman, 2002).

Planning

At the start of lessons, students can set specific, achievable learning goals. For example, in a Year 9 science lesson on chemical reactions, students might write down what they aim to understand, such as identifying reactants and products. Teachers model how to break complex tasks into manageable steps, showing how to plan experiments or investigations. Goal-setting encourages focus and intentional learning while providing a reference point for reflection and self-assessment.

Connecting

Students link new knowledge to prior learning or real-world contexts. For instance, a pupil studying climate change may connect global patterns to local environmental initiatives, reinforcing understanding and relevance. Making connections helps learners recognise the purpose of learning, deepens comprehension and enhances engagement and emotional satisfaction. For disadvantaged students, connecting concepts to real-life contexts can make learning more meaningful and reduce cognitive overload.

Monitoring and checking

Students are prompted to self-assess during tasks. For example, in history lessons, pupils can compare their interpretations of primary sources with learning objectives, noting areas of confusion. Teachers provide checklists or reflective prompts to guide the process, supporting learners in identifying errors, testing assumptions and adjusting strategies. Monitoring develops self-awareness and reduces dependence on teacher direction, fostering independence and resilience (Flavell, 1979).

Evaluating

At the end of lessons or units, pupils reflect on which strategies worked well and which could be improved. Peer discussion sessions can scaffold evaluation, allowing students to consider alternative perspectives and critically assess their own approaches. Evaluation encourages a growth mindset, supporting the idea that learning is iterative and that effort and strategy adaptation lead to success (Dweck, 2006).

Lesson example: Secondary classroom

In a Year 10 English lesson, students analyse two contrasting interpretations of a Shakespearean scene. The teacher models thinking aloud, questioning evidence and considering alternative interpretations. Students then plan their analysis, monitor comprehension during writing and evaluate the effectiveness of their arguments at the end. The reflective process fosters critical thinking, promotes self-regulation and reduces anxiety about producing a 'right' answer. Disadvantaged learners particularly benefit from structured support, which allows them to engage confidently with challenging tasks and develop strategies for independent learning.

Classroom snapshot: Year 4 literacy and wellbeing

At a primary school serving a socioeconomically disadvantaged community, the Year 4 teacher observed that many students were anxious about writing tasks, lacked confidence and often disengaged. Inspired by research linking metacognition to wellbeing (Mughal, 2021; Zimmerman, 2002), the teacher aimed to implement strategies that promoted self-regulation, resilience and positive emotional engagement.

The teacher introduced explicit metacognitive instruction using an expanded framework: 'Plan, Connect, Check, Monitor, Reflect':

- **Plan:** Students used visual 'story maps' to outline the beginning, middle and end of their narrative.
- **Connect:** Pupils were encouraged to link ideas to prior knowledge, personal experiences or other stories they had read. For example, a student writing about a character's journey connected it to a story they previously enjoyed.

- **Check:** Pupils used simple checklists to verify sentence clarity, spelling and structure, as well as whether ideas flowed logically.
- **Monitor:** During writing, students monitored their progress, asking themselves if their sentences made sense and whether they were following their plan.
- **Reflect:** After completing tasks, students responded to prompts such as: *'What did I do well?'* and *'Which strategy helped me overcome challenges?'*.

The teachers modelled thinking aloud, showing how to connect ideas, revise work and check progress. Peer discussions were included to encourage collaborative reflection, normalise mistakes and share strategies.

Over six weeks, students demonstrated greater engagement, reduced anxiety and increased confidence in writing. Reflection journals showed that pupils could articulate their strategy use, monitor progress and evaluate the effectiveness of their work. Social interactions improved, with students discussing connections between ideas and celebrating effort, fostering a supportive classroom culture.

The teacher concluded that embedding Connect and Check into metacognitive instruction enhanced both academic outcomes and emotional wellbeing, particularly for disadvantaged learners. Next steps include integrating daily short reflection and connection activities across all subjects and training teaching assistants to consistently scaffold metacognitive practices, helping students internalise these strategies for independent learning.

Classroom snapshot: Year 10 history and wellbeing

In a secondary school with a high proportion of disadvantaged learners, the Year 10 history teacher observed students feeling stressed when interpreting primary sources and writing essays. Research on metacognition and wellbeing (EEF, 2022; Zimmerman, 2002) inspired the implementation of strategies to develop self-regulation, critical thinking and emotional resilience.

Below, we refer to an expanded version of the familiar PCCME cycle. While teachers may be used to working with Plan–Connect–Check–Monitor–Evaluate, the teacher featured here was intentionally applying the full cognitive and pedagogical cycle: Plan, Connect, Monitor, Check, Analyse, Synthesise, Evaluate. These additional stages surface the thinking moves that often occur implicitly, allowing us to examine them more explicitly and purposefully.

- **Plan:** Students set specific learning goals, e.g. identifying bias in sources.
- **Connect:** Pupils linked new information to prior knowledge, current events or broader historical themes.
- **Monitor:** Students tracked comprehension and noted points of confusion during tasks.
- **Check:** Checklists were used to verify accuracy, structure and alignment with learning objectives.
- **Analyse:** Pupils critically examined evidence, considering source reliability and alternative interpretations.
- **Synthesise:** Students combined insights from multiple sources to form balanced arguments.
- **Evaluate:** Reflection prompts encouraged pupils to assess the effectiveness of their strategies and emotional responses.

Teachers modelled metacognitive processes, demonstrating how to integrate analysis and synthesis with ongoing monitoring and evaluation. Peer discussions supported collaborative thinking and normalised learning challenges.

Within two months, students improved analytical skills, persistence and confidence. They could connect new knowledge to prior learning, check accuracy, analyse multiple perspectives and synthesise information to produce coherent arguments. Reflection activities showed improved emotional regulation, reduced stress and stronger engagement.

The teacher concluded that combining Analysis and Synthesis with Connect, Check and Reflection significantly improved academic performance and wellbeing for disadvantaged learners. Next steps include embedding these strategies across all subjects, offering workshops on self-regulation and tracking both academic and wellbeing outcomes for long-term evaluation.

While the example above demonstrates the full 'Plan, Connect, Monitor, Check, Analyse, Synthesise, Evaluate' framework, it is important to note that this approach can be adapted to suit different contexts and learner needs. The 'Check' phase, for instance, can be positioned either before or after 'Monitor' depending on the task and the students' familiarity with the process. Some teachers may find it more effective to encourage students to check their initial understanding or plan before monitoring their ongoing progress, while others may integrate checking as part of the monitoring process itself.

By embedding metacognitive strategies across primary and secondary classrooms, teachers provide disadvantaged students with the tools to regulate learning, manage challenges and develop resilience. Strategies such as visual scaffolds, guided reflection, structured journals and collaborative discussion create a supportive environment that nurtures both academic and emotional development. These approaches equip pupils with lifelong skills, enabling them to navigate both classroom challenges and broader life stressors, fostering independence, confidence and wellbeing (EEF, 2022; Mughal, 2021; Zimmerman, 2002).

Outcomes of explicit metacognitive instruction

Research consistently highlights that explicitly teaching metacognitive strategies has profound benefits for students' academic performance, self-efficacy and overall wellbeing, particularly for those from disadvantaged backgrounds (EEF, 2022; Zimmerman, 2002). Metacognition enables learners to plan, monitor, evaluate and reflect on their learning processes. When students are taught these skills directly, they gain a greater sense of control over their learning, which fosters confidence, resilience and persistence in the face of challenges.

For disadvantaged students, who may face external stressors such as limited access to learning resources, unstable home environments or socioeconomic pressures, metacognitive strategies are particularly transformative. Explicit instruction provides these learners with structured tools to navigate academic tasks, manage frustration and develop adaptive coping strategies (Durlak et al., 2011; Reiss, 2013). For example, by learning to plan steps before starting a task, a pupil can break complex problems into manageable parts, reducing cognitive overload and anxiety. Similarly, regular opportunities to monitor progress and check understanding allow students to identify errors early and adjust their approach, supporting both learning and emotional regulation.

Embedding reflection and metacognitive practices across the curriculum also creates a classroom culture where mistakes are seen as learning opportunities rather than failures. In a primary literacy lesson, pupils might use 'planning boxes' to outline their writing and then reflect on what worked well and what could be improved. In secondary classrooms, students can evaluate their problem-solving strategies in mathematics or critically assess interpretations in history lessons. These structured reflection practices reinforce self-efficacy, as students recognise their ability to overcome challenges and develop independent learning skills (Mughal, 2021).

Furthermore, explicit metacognitive instruction contributes to improved wellbeing by enhancing self-regulation and reducing academic stress. Students who can plan, monitor and evaluate their learning are better equipped to manage setbacks, sustain effort and maintain motivation over time (Dweck, 2006; Zimmerman, 2002). For disadvantaged learners, these benefits are particularly significant, as metacognitive skills can compensate for reduced support outside school and provide a sense of agency in environments where students may otherwise feel powerless. Over time, the development of metacognition fosters resilience, emotional stability and a growth mindset, creating a reinforcing cycle in which enhanced learning success and improved wellbeing mutually support one another (EEF, 2022).

Ultimately, the outcomes of explicit metacognitive instruction extend far beyond academic achievement. By teaching students to think critically about how they learn, to recognise and correct errors and to reflect on their strategies, educators equip learners with lifelong skills for managing both cognitive and emotional challenges. These skills are essential for fostering confident, self-regulated and resilient students who are prepared not only for academic success but also for personal growth and wellbeing throughout life.

Conclusion

Explicitly teaching metacognition in schools is not merely an enhancement to classroom practice – it is a fundamental approach to fostering both academic success and emotional resilience. Metacognition, or the ability to think about one's own thinking, equips students with the tools to plan, monitor, evaluate and adjust their learning. For disadvantaged learners, who often face barriers such as limited access to learning resources, external stressors and fewer opportunities for structured support, these strategies are particularly transformative (Mughal, 2021; Zimmerman, 2002).

The dual benefit of metacognitive instruction lies in its ability to simultaneously strengthen cognitive and emotional skills. Academically, students become more independent and effective learners, able to break down complex tasks, identify effective strategies and evaluate the success of their approaches (Flavell, 1979). Emotionally, students gain self-efficacy and resilience. When learners recognise that setbacks are part of the learning process and that strategies can be adapted to overcome challenges, they develop confidence and a sense of control over their own learning journey (Dweck, 2006; EEF, 2022).

For teachers, the call to action is clear: integrate metacognitive strategies deliberately and consistently across the curriculum. Structured lesson designs should include clear learning goals, step-by-step guidance and opportunities for reflection. Reflective prompts encourage students to monitor their progress, identify challenges and evaluate their strategies. For example, in a Year 5 literacy lesson, pupils can plan their story structure, monitor word choice during writing and reflect on how effectively their story conveys meaning. In secondary classrooms, students can use metacognitive strategies to analyse sources in history, plan scientific investigations or evaluate problem-solving methods in mathematics.

Collaborative discussions are another powerful tool. Peer reflection encourages students to articulate their thinking, learn from others' strategies and normalise the experience of encountering difficulty. Visual scaffolds, such as learning ladders, checklists and 'thinking boxes', provide tangible reminders of the steps involved in metacognitive processes and can be especially supportive for disadvantaged learners who may require more explicit guidance.

By prioritising metacognition alongside wellbeing, teachers help students become resilient, self-regulated learners capable of navigating both academic and life challenges. Schools that embed these practices create a culture where mistakes are viewed as opportunities for growth, reflection is routine and learners develop both competence and confidence. This is particularly crucial for disadvantaged students, for whom structured strategies and supportive classroom environments can offset external disadvantages and equip them with lifelong learning skills (Norman et al., 2023; Reiss, 2013).

The message for educators is unequivocal: teaching metacognition explicitly is not an optional enhancement – it is essential. Every lesson should provide opportunities for students to plan, monitor, check, connect and evaluate their learning. By doing so, teachers do more than improve test scores; they empower students to understand how they learn, regulate their thinking and build resilience that extends far beyond the classroom. The integration of metacognition into everyday teaching is a practical, evidence-based pathway to fostering both academic achievement and emotional wellbeing, preparing students for lifelong success.

Implementation checkpoint: Creating conditions which support wellbeing

Evaluate your current practice:

✓ I explicitly teach the connection between metacognitive strategies and emotional regulation.

✓ Pupils know that feeling stuck or confused is normal and signals a need for a new strategy.

✓ I use language that combines growth mindset with metacognitive strategies.

✓ Pupils have regular opportunities to reflect on their learning and emotional experiences.

✓ I model managing my own frustration or confusion metacognitively.

✓ When pupils express anxiety or helplessness, I guide them to metacognitive strategies rather than just offering reassurance.

✓ I celebrate pupils using strategies to overcome difficulties, not just getting correct answers.

✓ Reflection activities help pupils develop self-awareness and self-regulation.

Choose one strategy to implement this month. How will you introduce it to pupils?

Key takeaways

- Metacognition and wellbeing are deeply connected; pupils who can regulate their thinking are better able to manage emotions.
- Teaching metacognitive strategies alongside emotional regulation helps disadvantaged pupils develop resilience.
- Reflection journals and regular prompts build self-awareness and provide pupils with tools to process challenges.
- Growth mindset language is more effective when combined with specific metacognitive strategies.
- Modelling self-compassion and strategic responses to errors shows pupils how to manage frustration.
- For disadvantaged pupils facing external stressors, metacognitive strategies provide a sense of control over their learning.
- Wellbeing improves when pupils shift from helpless ('*I can't*') to strategic ('*What strategy could help?*').

Reflection prompts

For educators:

- How do I currently support pupils' emotional wellbeing during challenging tasks?
- Do I explicitly teach the link between thinking strategies and emotional regulation?
- What opportunities exist for pupils to reflect on their learning experiences?
- How do I respond when pupils express anxiety, frustration or helplessness?

For school leaders:

- How does our school culture support both metacognition and wellbeing?
- What continuing professional development exists around teaching metacognitive strategies for emotional regulation?
- Do our wellbeing interventions incorporate metacognitive approaches?
- How do we measure the impact of metacognitive teaching on pupil wellbeing?

Next steps

- Introduce one 'power phrase' that combines growth mindset with metacognitive strategy to your class this week.
- Model managing your own frustration or confusion metacognitively during a lesson.
- Implement a simple weekly reflection prompt focused on both learning and emotions.
- When a pupil expresses anxiety or helplessness, guide them through a metacognitive question sequence.
- Create a visual display linking emotions (frustration, anxiety, confusion) to helpful metacognitive strategies.
- Share with colleagues one example of a pupil using metacognition to manage their emotional response to a challenge.

10 Metacognition and revision

Revision is a critical stage in the learning process, yet many students approach it passively, often rereading notes or memorising content without fully engaging with their understanding. Metacognition offers a framework to transform revision from a mechanical task into an active, strategic process (Flavell, 1979; Zimmerman, 2002). By teaching students to think about *how* they revise, educators can help them identify gaps in understanding, apply effective strategies and monitor their progress, ultimately improving both academic performance and confidence.

At its core, metacognitive revision involves three interrelated processes: planning, monitoring and evaluating. During planning, students set clear revision goals, decide which topics require more attention and select appropriate strategies. Monitoring requires students to continually assess their comprehension and progress. Finally, evaluation involves reflecting on the effectiveness of their revision strategies. This reflective cycle promotes self-regulation and a deeper, more durable understanding of the material.

Metacognitive approaches are particularly valuable for disadvantaged learners, who may have fewer opportunities to develop effective study habits independently and often face challenges such as limited access to educational resources, inconsistent support at home or interruptions in schooling. Research indicates that explicit instruction in metacognitive strategies can enhance not only academic outcomes but also students' confidence, resilience and sense of control over their learning (Education Endowment Foundation, 2022; Mughal, 2021). By learning to regulate their own thinking, these students can make the most of the time and materials available, improving understanding and retention even under challenging circumstances.

In this chapter, we explore how metacognitive principles can be applied to revision, providing practical strategies and evidence for primary and secondary students. We examine the research supporting the link between metacognition and effective study, and provide guidance on scaffolding revision activities to maximise student engagement and learning.

Understanding metacognition in revision

Metacognition enables learners to plan how they approach a task, monitor their understanding and evaluate their progress. Students who develop metacognitive skills can identify what they know, recognise gaps in their understanding and adjust their strategies accordingly (Flavell, 1979; Schraw & Dennison, 1994). For disadvantaged learners, who may have fewer external supports such as tutoring or parental guidance, metacognition allows them to take ownership of their learning.

Revision complements metacognition by providing structured opportunities to consolidate knowledge and correct misconceptions. Rather than passive repetition, effective revision involves deliberate reflection and strategy use. Techniques such as summarising material in one's own words, self-testing or creating concept maps help learners actively engage with content and identify gaps in understanding (Zimmerman, 2002). Importantly, these strategies do not require expensive resources; students can use simple tools such as paper, pen or verbal discussion with peers or family members.

The combination of metacognition and revision is particularly valuable for disadvantaged learners because it fosters autonomy and resilience. With limited access to teachers or tutors, these students must often rely on self-directed learning. Metacognitive revision enables them to plan study sessions, select effective strategies and monitor their own progress. Over time, these practices not only strengthen comprehension but also build confidence and a sense of ownership over learning.

Applying the PCCME framework to revision

As explored in Chapter 5, the PCCME framework – Plan, Connect, Check, Monitor, Evaluate – provides a structured approach to metacognitive learning. This framework is equally powerful when applied specifically to revision contexts, where students must independently consolidate and deepen their understanding of previously taught material.

In revision, the Connect phase takes on particular importance. Rather than connecting new learning to prior knowledge (as in initial teaching), during revision students connect material across topics, identifying patterns and relationships that may not have been apparent during first teaching. For instance, a student revising science might connect the concept of energy transfer across different contexts – thermal insulation, electrical circuits and food chains – recognising the underlying principles that link these apparently separate topics.

For disadvantaged learners, explicit instruction in making these connections during revision is crucial. These students may have experienced fragmented teaching or missed lessons, making it difficult to see how concepts relate. By teaching connection-making as a deliberate revision strategy – using prompts such as *'Where else have I seen this idea?'* or *'How does this link to what I learned in another topic?'* – teachers help students build the coherent understanding necessary for success.

The PCCME framework in revision contexts works as follows:

- **Plan:** Students identify which topics need revision, set specific goals ('I will be able to explain three causes of World War I'), and decide which strategies to use.

- **Connect:** Students link concepts across topics, relate new understanding to prior learning and identify patterns or themes. This is where deep learning occurs.

- **Check:** Students verify their understanding through self-testing, checking against success criteria or using mark schemes to assess their work.

- **Monitor:** Students track their progress during revision sessions, noting which areas are becoming clearer and which remain confusing.

- **Evaluate:** Students reflect on which revision strategies were most effective and plan how to revise similar material in future.

Practical metacognitive revision strategies

Implementing metacognition in revision provides both structure and autonomy for disadvantaged students. The following strategies can be integrated across subjects and adapted for different age groups:

- **Goal-oriented planning:** Breaking revision into specific, achievable goals – such as 'summarise three key concepts in physics today' – helps maintain focus and reduces cognitive overload. Scheduling regular, short revision sessions rather than long, unstructured periods ensures consistent engagement with content.

- **Summarising:** Condensing information into one's own words captures key ideas and forces active engagement with the material. For example, after reading a chapter, a student might write a short summary highlighting the main points, creating a concise resource for quick review.

- **Self-explanation and peer discussion:** Articulating reasoning or steps in one's own words, either verbally or in writing, reinforces understanding. Peer discussion extends this strategy by encouraging learners to teach concepts to others. For disadvantaged students who may have fewer opportunities for tutoring, these strategies provide low-cost methods of consolidating knowledge.

- **Concept mapping and visualisation:** Visual strategies such as concept maps or diagrams help learners organise and connect ideas. For students with gaps in prior knowledge, mapping key concepts and their relationships provides a scaffold for understanding complex information.

- **Monitoring and reflection:** Self-monitoring helps learners assess comprehension and adjust study methods. After each study session, learners can ask: *'Which parts did I understand well?'*, *'Which need more work?'*. Reflection builds awareness of strengths and weaknesses, improves strategy use and fosters autonomy.

- **Retrieval practice:** Actively recalling information from memory strengthens retention and identifies gaps. This can take the form of isolated retrieval (recalling without cues, such as flashcard self-testing) or embedded retrieval (retrieving knowledge within meaningful contexts, such as summarising while reading).

Retrieval practice

Retrieval practice focuses on actively recalling information rather than simply reviewing it. By pulling knowledge from memory, we strengthen it, making it less likely to be forgotten. Two types of retrieval practice – isolated and embedded retrieval – have been shown to significantly enhance learning outcomes, particularly for disadvantaged students (Agarwal et al., 2020; Mughal, 2020).

Isolated retrieval

Isolated retrieval refers to recalling information without contextual cues or prompts. It is often associated with traditional testing formats, such as answering questions from memory, free recall exercises or self-testing with flashcards. The strength of isolated retrieval lies in its ability to create desirable difficulty, which enhances long-term retention. For disadvantaged students, isolated retrieval is particularly valuable because it encourages independent engagement with content that may not have been reinforced at home or through formal instruction. By actively reconstructing knowledge, these learners can identify specific gaps in understanding, providing a structured approach to bridging educational inequities.

Embedded retrieval

Embedded retrieval integrates retrieval practice within meaningful learning contexts. Learners retrieve knowledge while engaged in activities such as reading, discussing or completing assignments. For instance, while reading a history text, a student might pause periodically to summarise key events or explain them aloud in their own words. For disadvantaged students, embedded retrieval is crucial because it links new information to familiar or practical contexts, helping them make sense of material that may initially seem abstract. It encourages comprehension, strengthens connections between new and prior knowledge, and promotes skill transfer.

Effective revision combines both isolated and embedded retrieval strategies. Learners can begin with isolated retrieval to pinpoint gaps and then use embedded retrieval to reinforce knowledge in applied contexts. Reflection after retrieval practice – such as evaluating which answers were accurate and why errors occurred – further strengthens metacognitive awareness.

Benefits of metacognitive revision

Metacognitive revision offers significant benefits for disadvantaged students, addressing barriers such as limited resources, inconsistent support and gaps in prior knowledge. By actively reflecting on understanding, monitoring progress and adjusting strategies, students engage in self-directed, strategic learning that leads to improved comprehension, retention and confidence.

Enhanced academic performance is one primary benefit. By regularly evaluating what they know and what they still need to master, students can prioritise areas that require the most attention. This targeted approach maximises the efficiency of study time and increases the likelihood of success in assessments. Additionally, metacognitive revision develops self-regulation and independent learning skills. Students learn to monitor their own progress, set achievable goals and evaluate the effectiveness of different learning strategies. This fosters autonomy and resilience, empowering students to take control of their educational journey.

Furthermore, metacognitive revision improves problem-solving and critical thinking. By reflecting on their thought processes and considering alternative strategies when encountering difficulties, students approach complex tasks with greater confidence and adaptability. Research demonstrates that learners who actively engage in monitoring and evaluating their study approaches are more likely to persist through challenges, reduce anxiety and develop lifelong learning habits (EEF, 2022; Zimmerman, 2002).

Metacognitive revision in practice

Reflection journals in mathematics

In a low-income secondary school, students preparing for mathematics exams struggled with problem-solving. Teachers introduced a metacognitive revision strategy in which students attempted problems, reflected on the methods they used, identified errors, and then adjusted strategies accordingly. Initially, many students wrote superficial entries because they lacked the foundational understanding to identify errors. Educators responded by providing structured prompts, such as *'Which step did I find most difficult?'* and *'Which formula did I forget to apply?'*. Over several weeks, students demonstrated improved accuracy, confidence and a deeper understanding of problem-solving techniques.

Literacy programme reflection logs

In a community literacy programme for disadvantaged adolescents, learners struggled with reading comprehension and vocabulary retention. Educators implemented reflection logs as part of metacognitive revision. Students recorded sections they understood, areas that were confusing, and strategies to improve comprehension. Learners often lacked private study spaces, so educators created group reflection sessions during programme hours and provided low-cost printed reflection sheets. Over time, learners became more independent, identifying gaps without constant teacher guidance. This process improved both reading fluency and comprehension scores while also increasing motivation and engagement.

Vocational training self-monitoring

In a vocational training programme for disadvantaged young adults, students needed to memorise procedures for workplace safety. Initially, learners were hesitant to use self-monitoring checklists, fearing that highlighting mistakes would reflect negatively on their abilities. Instructors encouraged gradual use of the checklists, emphasising that reflection is a tool for improvement rather than evaluation. Over time, students gained confidence in evaluating their own performance, internalised procedures more efficiently, reduced mistakes during practical assessments and developed stronger independent problem-solving skills.

Metacognitive moment: Managing test anxiety through metacognition

Before mock GCSEs, Miss Lee noticed many pupils expressing anxiety. Rather than just offering general reassurance, she taught a metacognitive approach to managing test stress:

'When you feel anxious during the exam, pause and ask yourself: What zone am I in? If you're panicking, take three slow breaths. Then ask: What do I know? What's the question really asking? What strategy will I try first? Breaking the problem down helps your brain shift from panic mode to problem-solving mode. That's using metacognition to manage your emotional state.'

She had pupils practice this with past papers, pausing deliberately when they felt stuck to rehearse the calming and strategic questions. Several pupils reported that this approach helped them stay calmer during actual exams.

Case study: Metacognition in revision for disadvantaged secondary students

Context and problem

At a secondary school serving a high proportion of socioeconomically disadvantaged students, teachers observed that many pupils struggled with independent revision ahead of their GCSE exams. Key issues included:

- **Poor strategy use:** Students' revision often involved passive rereading of notes rather than active learning.

- **Lack of monitoring:** Learners were not good at judging what they understood versus what they didn't, so they wasted time on material they already knew.

- **Limited feedback and reflection:** After mock exams, few students reflected on their errors or planned how to improve.

- **Low self-regulation:** Many students lacked confidence in approaching revision; some felt overwhelmed or gave up easily, especially when working alone at home.

These problems were contributing to underperformance: disadvantaged students were less likely to improve between mocks and finals.

Intervention: Metacognitive revision programme

To address this, the school introduced a *structured metacognitive revision programme* in the year leading up to the exams. The intervention combined teacher training, student workshops and regular metacognitive reflection. Key components included the following.

Teacher training

- Teachers (especially in core subjects: maths, English, sciences) received professional development on metacognitive strategies for revision – planning, monitoring, evaluating.

- They learned how to scaffold revision sessions and model self-regulation and metacognitive talk (think-aloud) during revision.

Student workshops

- Students attended a series of workshops (in tutor time or after school) where they learned metacognitive revision strategies, such as:

  - **Goal-setting and planning:** Breaking down revision into manageable tasks, setting specific goals (e.g. 'I will master topic X by Friday').

  - **Self-testing and retrieval practice:** Using flashcards, practice questions and quizzing themselves rather than passive reading.

  - **Confidence-rating:** After attempting a revision question, students rated their confidence in their answer, helping them monitor which topics needed more work.

  - **Error analysis:** After the mock or practice exam, students reflected on their mistakes, asked *'Why did I get that wrong?'* and planned corrective strategies.

  - **Revision journals/exam wrappers:** Students completed 'exam wrappers' – short reflective exercises after mock papers, where they wrote about what they found difficult, which strategies helped and what they would change next time.

Ongoing support and metacognitive prompts

- During weekly revision sessions, teachers prompted metacognitive reflection: e.g. *'Which topics are you most confident in?'*, *'Which are you least confident in?'*, *'How will you revise the weaker topics?'*.

- Self-assessment checklists and metacognitive guides were provided to students (e.g. 'Stop and Think' prompt cards).

- After each mock exam, students completed structured reflection and then created a revised revision plan based on their reflections.

Outcomes and impact

Following the implementation of the metacognitive revision programme, several positive outcomes emerged.

Improved exam performance

- Students on average made greater improvements between their first and second mock exams compared to previous cohorts.

- Teachers reported that the most marked gains came from students who engaged in self-testing and confidence-rating; these students more accurately identified their weak areas and focused revision more productively.

Better self-regulation and agency

- Students reported feeling more in control of their revision. In surveys, many said that the exam wrapper reflections helped them *understand how they learn*.
- Confidence among lower-attaining students rose; by reflecting on their mistakes and planning how to improve, they felt less overwhelmed and more capable.

Equity gains

- The improvement was especially significant for students from disadvantaged backgrounds; those who historically struggled with exam preparation showed disproportionately large gains in metacognitive awareness, according to teacher feedback.
- The use of structured self-reflection and metacognitive prompts helped 'level the playing field', giving all students access to strategies that more advantaged or self-regulated learners might already be using.

Sustainable behaviour change

- By the end of the academic year, many students began to adopt metacognitive strategies more independently. Teachers noted that fewer students needed to be prompted weekly to reflect – they were becoming more self-driven.
- Some students continued to use revision journals and self-testing beyond mock exams, integrating these habits into their regular study routines.

Analysis and lessons learned

- **Why metacognition helped in revision:** Revision is not just about content – it's about *how* students are thinking, remembering and regulating their own study. By making metacognition explicit (confidence ratings, error analysis, planning), students gained tools to monitor and direct their revision more efficiently.

- **Teacher modelling is crucial:** The success of this programme hinged on teachers modelling metacognitive reflection themselves. When teachers shared how they think about planning, checking and revising, students were more likely to adopt those behaviours.

- **Structured reflection matters:** Without structured post-exam reflection (exam wrappers), many students would not naturally reflect on their mistakes or plan how to improve. The reflection phase is essential for metacognitive growth.

- **Equity implications:** Disadvantaged students are less likely to have metacognitive habits built from prior educational or home experiences. Coaching them explicitly in these habits helps close that gap.

- **Sustainability:** For metacognitive revision strategies to stick, they need to be embedded in regular routines. Weekly prompts, consistent use of reflection tools and fading scaffolds over time support long-term behavioural change.

- **Challenges:** Some students initially resisted 'extra work' of reflection, seeing it as time-consuming. Teachers had to emphasise the payoff: better exam performance, more efficient revision and less wasted time.

Recommendations for schools

- **Implement metacognitive revision training:** Build workshops for students focused on metacognitive strategies specifically for revision (goal-setting, retrieval practice, confidence rating, error analysis).

- **Train teachers:** Provide professional development so teachers can model metacognitive talk during revision sessions.

- **Use exam wrappers:** Introduce structured reflection tools for after mock exams (or any assessment) so students can reflect, plan and adapt.

- **Embed prompts in routine:** Use weekly class or tutor-time prompts to help students monitor their confidence, progress and strategy use.

- **Track impact:** Monitor improvements in mock exam scores, but also survey students' metacognitive awareness over time to assess how their self-regulation evolves.

- **Fade scaffolding:** Gradually reduce support (e.g. from guided reflection to independent revision planning) to build student autonomy.

Connection to broader evidence

- The Education Endowment Foundation (EEF) highlights that metacognitive strategies are effective for disadvantaged pupils *especially when explicitly taught* (EEF, n.d.).

- A UK-based study found that many students use low utility strategies for independent study in science revision; more effective metacognitive strategies (like self-testing) are underused (Sultana et al., 2025).

- The EEF has published real case studies showing how schools used metacognitive strategies for independent revision with success for students who needed more structured support (EEF, n.d.a).

Challenges and considerations

While metacognitive revision offers substantial benefits, implementing it effectively for disadvantaged students presents unique challenges. These learners often encounter structural and personal barriers, including limited access to resources, inconsistent support at home, large class sizes and gaps in prior knowledge.

One significant challenge is gaps in foundational knowledge. Metacognitive revision relies on learners' ability to evaluate their own understanding accurately. Students with interrupted or inconsistent schooling may lack the prior knowledge necessary to assess their understanding, leading to ineffective reflection or frustration. A student may believe they understand a concept when, in fact, they have overlooked critical elements.

Another challenge is limited access to resources and structured support. Disadvantaged students may not have quiet spaces to study, sufficient materials or consistent guidance from teachers or tutors. Metacognitive revision often requires tools such as notebooks, checklists or practice questions, as well as time to engage in reflection. Without these resources, learners may struggle to implement strategies consistently.

A further challenge is motivation and self-efficacy. Disadvantaged students may have experienced repeated academic setbacks or systemic barriers, leading to low confidence and a reluctance to engage in self-reflection. Metacognitive revision requires persistence, honest self-assessment and the willingness to address mistakes – tasks that can be intimidating for learners who fear failure or have low expectations of their capabilities.

When implementing metacognitive revision, educators should consider several key factors:

- **Provide structured guidance:** Include prompts, templates and scaffolding to help learners identify gaps and develop strategies.
- **Ensure accessibility:** Tools and activities should be low-cost and accessible, such as reflection journals, checklists or peer discussions.
- **Connect to lived experiences:** Linking learning to students' personal experiences and real-world contexts increases engagement and relevance.
- **Support emotional wellbeing:** Recognise the emotional and motivational aspects of learning, encouraging learners to view mistakes as opportunities for growth.

By carefully addressing these considerations, educators can empower disadvantaged learners to engage effectively in metacognitive revision, develop independent learning skills, improve academic outcomes and build confidence, resilience and lifelong learning capabilities.

Conclusion

Metacognitive revision strategies play a crucial role in effective learning. When the PCCME framework introduced in Chapter 5 is applied specifically to revision contexts, it provides disadvantaged students with a structured approach to consolidating and deepening their understanding. The Connect phase, in particular, takes on new importance during revision, as students must link concepts across topics and identify patterns that may not have been apparent during initial teaching.

Isolated retrieval strengthens memory and highlights gaps in understanding, while embedded retrieval situates recall within meaningful contexts, supporting application and integration of knowledge. Together with planning, monitoring and evaluation, these practices enhance comprehension, retention and metacognitive awareness, allowing learners to engage with revision purposefully, monitor their understanding and adjust strategies effectively.

While challenges exist – including gaps in foundational knowledge, limited resources and low self-efficacy – structured scaffolding, accessible tools and supportive learning environments enable success. By applying the PCCME framework to revision and prioritising both active retrieval and meaningful connections, educators can help students revise strategically, develop self-directed learning skills and approach challenges with confidence, fostering long-term academic success and lifelong learning.

Key takeaways

- Metacognitive revision transforms revision from passive review into an active, strategic process.
- The PCCME framework (Plan, Connect, Check, Monitor, Evaluate) supports structured, self-directed revision.
- Retrieval practice – both isolated and embedded – enhances memory and highlights gaps in understanding.
- Disadvantaged students benefit from explicit instruction in planning, monitoring and evaluating their revision strategies.
- Metacognitive revision builds confidence, resilience and long-term learning habits.

Reflection prompts

For students:

- What revision strategy helped me understand this topic best?
- How do I know I'm ready to move on from a topic?
- What do I do when I get stuck during revision?
- How can I connect this topic to others I've studied?

For educators:

- How do I model effective revision strategies for my pupils?
- Are my students able to explain how they revise, not just what they revise?
- What support do disadvantaged pupils need to revise independently and confidently?

Implementation checkpoint: Getting ready for revision

✓ I have introduced the PCCME framework as a tool for structuring revision.

✓ Pupils are using both isolated and embedded retrieval strategies.

✓ I provide scaffolds (e.g. checklists, prompts, templates) to support metacognitive revision.

✓ Pupils reflect on their revision strategies and adjust them over time.

✓ I have identified and addressed barriers to effective revision for disadvantaged learners.

Next steps

- Introduce a revision journal where pupils track their strategies, challenges and progress.
- Model a revision session using the PCCME framework.
- Create a bank of low-cost, high-impact revision tools (e.g. flashcards, concept maps, self-testing prompts).
- Run a workshop or assembly on metacognitive revision strategies before exam periods.
- Encourage peer-led revision groups that include structured reflection and strategy sharing.

11 The path forward

As we reach the culmination of this exploration into metacognition and its transformative potential for disadvantaged learners, it is essential to reflect not only on what has been learned but also on how this knowledge can shape a more equitable future. Metacognition offers learners a toolkit for self-awareness, strategic planning and adaptive problem-solving. For students facing systemic challenges, these skills are not merely academic enhancements; they are lifelines that empower individuals to navigate obstacles, take ownership of their learning, and cultivate resilience in the face of adversity.

This concluding chapter moves beyond theory, offering a forward-looking perspective on implementation and impact. It seeks to bridge insight with action, outlining practical pathways for educators, policymakers and learners themselves to embed metacognitive practices in classrooms, curricula and daily routines. By reflecting on both successes and challenges presented in earlier chapters, we aim to provide a roadmap for sustainable growth, where every learner – regardless of background – can develop the cognitive strategies needed to thrive.

Ultimately, this chapter envisions a future in which metacognition serves as a cornerstone of equitable education. It is an invitation to reimagine learning environments that prioritise reflection, strategy and self-directed growth, ensuring that disadvantaged learners are not merely participants in education but empowered architects of their own academic journeys and life trajectories.

Research summary: Carol S. Dweck's *Mindset: The New Psychology of Success* (2006)

Methodology: Carol S. Dweck's *Mindset: The New Psychology of Success* (2006) builds on extensive psychological research, including longitudinal studies, experimental designs and observational analyses, to examine how beliefs about intelligence and ability affect motivation, learning and achievement. The book integrates empirical evidence with real-world examples from education, sports, business and personal development. Dweck also presents case studies and classroom interventions to demonstrate how mindsets manifest in behaviour and performance, offering both qualitative and quantitative support for her framework.

Key findings: Dweck identifies two primary mindsets: the fixed mindset and the growth mindset. Individuals with a fixed mindset perceive intelligence and abilities as static, often avoiding challenges, giving up easily and viewing effort as futile. They may feel threatened by others' success and conceal failures to protect self-image. In contrast, individuals with a growth mindset believe abilities can be developed through effort and learning. This perspective fosters resilience, persistence and the view that failure is an opportunity for growth. Research shows that adopting a growth mindset enhances motivation, achievement and adaptability across academics, sports, business and relationships.

Practical implications: The book emphasises strategies to cultivate a growth mindset, particularly in educational contexts. Educators, parents and leaders can encourage growth by praising effort, strategy and progress rather than innate traits. Language and feedback are critical in shaping beliefs about ability, shifting focus from outcomes to learning processes. Implementing these practices can promote lifelong learning, help close achievement gaps and empower individuals to reach their full potential in diverse contexts.

The imperative for equity in education

As education advances, the imperative for equity in learning becomes more pronounced. Yet, true equity extends beyond merely providing access to resources, technology or standardised curricula. At its core, equitable education empowers every learner to understand and regulate their own learning processes.

This empowerment is where metacognition – the awareness and control of one's thinking – plays a transformative role. Developing metacognitive skills enables students to take ownership of their learning journey, fostering independence, resilience and adaptability. These qualities are essential not only for academic success but also for lifelong learning in an ever-changing world.

Metacognition involves a learner's ability to monitor their cognitive processes, evaluate their understanding, and adjust strategies to enhance learning outcomes. This self-regulatory capacity equips students to identify when they do not understand something, seek appropriate help and persist through challenges. For disadvantaged learners, who often face additional social, emotional and academic obstacles, metacognition offers a crucial toolkit to navigate these barriers effectively. When learners develop metacognitive awareness, they shift from passive recipients of information to active participants in their education, capable of directing their efforts and adapting to new demands.

Embedding metacognitive practices within educational frameworks is thus essential for promoting equity. This requires intentional teaching that makes thinking visible and encourages reflection as a regular part of classroom routines. Strategies such as learning journals, reflective questioning, peer feedback and self-assessment prompts provide students with structured opportunities to practice metacognitive skills. However, these strategies must be carefully scaffolded to ensure they are accessible to all students, particularly those who may lack prior experience with reflective learning or confidence in their abilities.

Moreover, a culture that values metacognition must be cultivated at multiple levels – within classrooms, schools and education systems. Teachers play a pivotal role by modelling metacognitive thinking, providing timely feedback and fostering safe environments where mistakes are viewed as learning opportunities. Systemic support in the form of professional development, curriculum design and assessment policies that prioritise metacognitive skills further reinforces this cultural shift.

The benefits of this approach extend far beyond academic achievement. Metacognitive skills contribute to the development of resilience, enabling learners to manage setbacks and persist with motivation. They foster independence, allowing students to take initiative and responsibility for their growth. Importantly, these skills prepare learners for lifelong learning, equipping them to adapt to new challenges and opportunities throughout their lives.

Understanding the potential of metacognition for equity

Metacognition, extensively defined by Flavell (1979), refers to the active monitoring and regulation of one's own cognitive processes. It encompasses a learner's ability to recognise gaps in their understanding, select effective strategies to address those gaps, evaluate their progress throughout the learning process and adapt their approaches as necessary. This self-regulatory capacity is fundamental for effective learning because it transforms students from passive recipients of information into active managers of their own educational journey. For disadvantaged learners – who frequently confront social, emotional and academic barriers – metacognition offers an essential toolkit. It empowers them to navigate challenges with greater agency, confidence and resilience, fostering independence and supporting sustained academic growth.

Despite its potential, the benefits of metacognition cannot be fully realised by simply understanding its theoretical foundations. The real challenge lies in translating this knowledge into accessible and responsive strategies that meet the diverse needs of all learners, especially those who are disadvantaged. Often, students from marginalised or under-resourced backgrounds do not have access to the scaffolding, encouragement or tools needed to develop metacognitive skills independently. Without intentional and thoughtful support, metacognition risks becoming another element that widens educational disparities rather than closes them. Those students who already benefit from supportive environments and prior knowledge of reflective practices are more likely to develop strong metacognitive skills, while disadvantaged learners may fall further behind.

The future of equitable education, therefore, hinges on embedding metacognitive development within teaching practice in ways that are inclusive, scaffolded and culturally responsive. Educators must move beyond merely delivering academic content and become facilitators of metacognitive growth. This requires explicitly modelling metacognitive strategies, guiding students through reflective thinking processes and monitoring their use of these strategies throughout the learning cycle. By making metacognition visible and accessible, teachers can help students internalise these skills, gradually fostering greater independence.

Scaffolding is particularly crucial in this context. Breaking down complex metacognitive processes into manageable steps, providing clear prompts and sentence starters, and using formative assessment tools can support disadvantaged learners in developing confidence and competence. Additionally, culturally responsive teaching acknowledges the diverse backgrounds and experiences students bring to the classroom, ensuring that metacognitive instruction connects with their realities and values their perspectives. This responsiveness strengthens engagement and relevance, further supporting metacognitive development.

Moreover, educational systems must invest in professional development for teachers to build their capacity to teach metacognition effectively and inclusively. System-wide support through curriculum design, assessment frameworks and resource allocation reinforces the priority of metacognitive skills. Integrating metacognition into learning goals and accountability measures signals its critical role in student success.

Building a culture of metacognitive growth

Creating a classroom culture that deeply values metacognition is a critical step towards fostering meaningful and equitable learning experiences. Such a culture encourages students to engage in consistent reflection, use metacognitive language regularly, interact with visible prompts and celebrate not just outcomes but the effort and strategic thinking involved in the learning process. This approach helps shift the focus from viewing intelligence as a fixed trait towards understanding learning as a dynamic, ongoing journey that involves trial, error and continuous adjustment. By normalising reflection and strategic thinking, educators can cultivate environments where students feel safe to take intellectual risks and develop self-regulation skills essential for academic and personal success.

In classrooms where metacognitive growth is actively prioritised, disadvantaged learners especially benefit. Research has shown that students from marginalised or under-resourced backgrounds often struggle with internalised beliefs about their academic capabilities, which can undermine motivation and persistence (Dweck, 2006). When educators create spaces that encourage reflection and recognise effort and strategy-use as markers of success, these learners begin to see themselves as capable thinkers and problem-solvers rather than victims of their circumstances. This reframing is foundational to fostering resilience and a growth mindset – concepts linked to increased motivation, engagement and academic persistence.

A culture that embraces metacognition makes learning visible and accessible, breaking down complex tasks into manageable steps while emphasising the value of monitoring one's own understanding and progress. Strategies like using metacognitive prompts on classroom walls, engaging students in reflective discussions and explicitly teaching the language of thinking support this culture.

These practices help students articulate their thought processes and identify effective learning strategies, empowering them to become more autonomous learners.

Moreover, celebrating metacognitive growth alongside academic achievement helps to reinforce the importance of effort, strategy and persistence. This recognition encourages students to take ownership of their learning and understand that setbacks are part of the process rather than signs of failure. Such an approach aligns with the principles of growth mindset theory, which emphasises that intelligence and abilities can be developed through dedication and hard work (Dweck, 2006). By integrating these ideas into the fabric of classroom culture, educators can help all students, and particularly disadvantaged learners, build the confidence needed to tackle challenges and sustain motivation over time.

Implementation guide

The future of effective education lies in equipping students with metacognitive skills – abilities to think about and regulate their own learning. To achieve this, educators must adopt a range of tools and strategies that make metacognition visible, explicit and manageable within the classroom. These strategies not only help students understand their current learning status but also guide them on how to progress, fostering greater ownership and control over their educational journeys.

- **Visual aids:** One essential set of tools includes learning ladders and progress maps. These visual aids help students identify where they stand in their learning and clearly outline the steps required to advance. By breaking down complex learning goals into smaller, achievable milestones, learners can better monitor their progress and feel motivated by incremental success.
- **Journals and logs:** Alongside the visual aids, metacognitive journals and learning logs encourage students to engage in regular reflection on their thinking and learning strategies. This habit of self-reflection deepens their awareness of what works, what doesn't, and why.

- **Exit tickets and prompts:** Exit tickets and metacognitive prompts serve as quick, formative assessments that prompt immediate self-evaluation. These tools help learners consider their understanding at the end of a lesson, making the invisible processes of thinking and learning visible.

- **Feedback and reflection:** Peer feedback and collaborative reflection also play a vital role, creating opportunities for dialogue about thinking. Discussing problem-solving approaches and reasoning with peers not only enhances metacognitive skills but builds a community of learners who support each other's growth.

- **Portfolios:** Digital portfolios provide a dynamic space to document and showcase ongoing metacognitive development, allowing students to see tangible evidence of their progress over time.

However, the true power of these tools is unlocked only when they are thoughtfully scaffolded – especially for disadvantaged learners who often face additional barriers to developing metacognitive skills independently. Scaffolding involves breaking down complex metacognitive processes into clear, manageable steps, using language that is accessible and relatable. Providing sentence starters, checklists or graphic organisers can guide learners in reflecting more effectively and confidently. Consistent support through teacher check-ins or peer mentoring ensures students receive timely feedback and encouragement, helping to build self-regulation incrementally.

Research by Paris and Paris (2003) highlights the importance of such scaffolding in fostering metacognitive development. They emphasise that metacognitive instruction must be explicit and supported by concrete tools to be effective, particularly for learners who might not have had prior exposure to reflective practices. By making metacognitive strategies accessible and responsive to students' needs, educators create pathways for all learners to gradually develop independence and resilience.

The role of educators and systems

Teachers are central to fostering metacognitive growth among students, acting as guides who model reflective thinking, create supportive environments and offer timely, constructive feedback. Their role goes beyond delivering content; it involves demonstrating how to think about learning itself, encouraging students to question their understanding, plan their approach and evaluate their progress. When teachers authentically integrate metacognitive practices into their instruction, students begin to see learning as an active, self-directed process rather than a passive reception of information.

To enable educators to fulfil this role effectively, professional development focused specifically on metacognitive instruction is essential. Such training equips teachers with both the theoretical understanding and practical strategies needed to embed metacognition across subjects and grade levels (Hattie & Timperley, 2007).

At the systemic level, embedding metacognition into educational policies and frameworks is critical for widespread impact. Curricula that explicitly incorporate metacognitive skills alongside content knowledge emphasise their value and encourage consistent practice. Likewise, assessments designed to measure not only academic achievement but also students' ability to reflect on their learning help reinforce metacognitive development as a priority. Resource allocation should also reflect this focus, with investments in technologies, materials and tools that facilitate reflective practices – such as digital portfolios, learning journals or metacognitive prompts – making these approaches more accessible, particularly in under-resourced schools.

Educational policies must also address structural factors that influence metacognitive growth. Smaller class sizes and collaborative teaching models enable teachers to provide personalised guidance and feedback, which are vital for developing metacognitive skills. When educators can spend more time with individual students, they can better scaffold reflective practices and respond to diverse learning needs. Furthermore, fostering partnerships with families and communities extends the support for metacognitive development beyond the classroom. When students receive consistent messages about the importance of reflection and self-regulation at home and in school, their motivation and capacity for independent learning are strengthened.

This holistic approach – integrating teacher training, policy reforms, resource support and community engagement – creates an ecosystem where metacognitive growth can flourish. As noted by Hattie and Timperley (2007), effective feedback and a culture of reflection are among the most powerful influences on student achievement. By prioritising metacognition at all levels of education, we move closer to a system that not only improves academic outcomes but also empowers learners with the skills they need for lifelong learning and success.

Metacognition as a catalyst for lifelong learning and social mobility

Metacognition extends far beyond academic achievement; it is a vital life skill that empowers individuals to navigate the complexities of modern life. The ability to monitor, evaluate and regulate one's own thinking cultivates essential competencies such as adaptability, critical thinking and effective problem-solving. These skills are indispensable in a rapidly changing world where learners must continuously adjust to new information, challenges and environments. For disadvantaged learners in particular, developing metacognitive skills can be transformative. It opens pathways to opportunities that may have previously seemed inaccessible, fostering social mobility and helping to break entrenched cycles of poverty and marginalisation.

As economies and societies evolve into increasingly knowledge-driven and interconnected systems, the demand for self-directed, lifelong learners intensifies. Today's students will face careers and challenges that do not yet exist, requiring the ability to think independently, reflect critically and adapt strategically. Embedding metacognitive growth within equitable education frameworks is therefore not just desirable but essential. It prepares all learners – regardless of their socioeconomic backgrounds – to succeed not only academically but in life beyond the classroom.

Achieving this vision calls for collective and coordinated action among all stakeholders in education. Teachers, school leaders, policymakers, researchers, families and communities must unite to prioritise metacognitive development as a fundamental right for every student. This commitment involves multiple concrete steps:

1 Investing in teacher professional development is crucial. Educators need targeted training that combines metacognitive instruction with culturally responsive teaching practices, ensuring they can meet the diverse needs of their learners effectively (King, 2018).

2 Curriculum design must explicitly integrate metacognitive skills, providing clear guidance and practical resources to support implementation. Without intentional embedding, metacognition risks becoming an afterthought rather than a core educational priority.

3 Equitable access to scaffolding tools and digital platforms that facilitate reflection and self-regulation is vital. Technology can play a pivotal

role in making metacognitive practices more accessible, especially for disadvantaged students who may lack other resources.

4   Cultivating classroom environments that value and celebrate metacognitive effort and resilience fosters a growth mindset culture. When students recognise that persistence, reflection and strategic adjustment are as important as correct answers, they develop the confidence to tackle complex tasks and learn from setbacks.

5   Engaging families and communities in understanding and supporting metacognitive practices creates a consistent and reinforcing ecosystem for learners, bridging home and school experiences.

6   Ongoing research is essential to continually refine metacognitive strategies and ensure they address the evolving needs of diverse learners. Collaboration between researchers and practitioners can generate evidence-based approaches that maximise impact and inclusivity.

By embracing this comprehensive approach, we can create an education system that not only imparts knowledge but equips all students with the metacognitive tools needed to thrive in a dynamic world.

A vision for the future

Metacognition offers a powerful framework for transforming education into an equitable environment where all students have the opportunity to succeed and thrive. Unlike traditional models that often emphasise passive reception of information, metacognition promotes active engagement with learning through reflection, self-awareness and regulation of one's own thinking processes. This shift is particularly crucial for disadvantaged learners, who frequently face systemic barriers that limit their access to effective learning strategies and the confidence needed to navigate academic challenges. Developing metacognitive skills equips these students not only with better academic outcomes but also with greater independence, resilience and the ability to adapt to new situations – skills that extend far beyond the classroom and into lifelong learning.

Embedding metacognitive development within education fosters a shift from viewing intelligence and ability as fixed traits to understanding learning as a dynamic process. When learners, especially those from marginalised backgrounds, are taught to monitor and adjust their thinking, they begin to see themselves as active agents in their education. This empowerment can break cycles of disadvantage by encouraging persistence, self-efficacy and a growth mindset. Moreover, metacognition supports critical thinking and problem-solving, which are essential competencies in the complex and rapidly evolving global landscape.

For education systems aiming to achieve true equity, prioritising metacognition is no longer optional but imperative. It requires a commitment at multiple levels: classroom practices, school leadership, policy design and resource allocation. Teachers must be equipped with training and tools to model and scaffold metacognitive strategies effectively, adapting them to meet diverse learner needs. Schools should cultivate cultures that value reflection, resilience and effort alongside achievement, providing ongoing support that encourages students to take ownership of their learning journeys.

Beyond schools, policies that integrate metacognitive skills into curricula and assessment frameworks send a clear message about their importance. Investments in technology and resources that support reflective learning practices can help bridge gaps in access, particularly for disadvantaged students. Finally, engaging families and communities in understanding and reinforcing metacognitive habits creates a consistent and supportive environment for learners to develop these skills holistically.

This vision of equitable education through metacognition aligns with the findings of Hattie and Donoghue (2016), who highlight that metacognitive strategies are among the most effective influences on student achievement. By shifting the focus to how students learn, rather than just what they learn, education becomes a transformative experience that fosters autonomy, critical awareness and lifelong adaptability.

In essence, metacognition is a gateway to educational equity and social justice. It is not merely an academic skill but a fundamental capability that empowers learners to realise their full potential. By embedding metacognitive growth at the heart of educational systems, we pave the way towards classrooms and communities where every student is valued, supported and prepared to succeed in a complex and changing world.

References

Abdelrahman, R. M. (2020), 'Metacognitive awareness and academic motivation as predictors of academic achievement', *Heliyon*, 6, (10), e05102. https://doi.org/10.1016/j.heliyon.2020.e05102

Agarwal, P. K., Roediger, H. L., McDaniel, M. A. and McDermott, K. B. (2020), 'How to use retrieval practice to improve learning', http://pdf.retrievalpractice.org/RetrievalPracticeGuide.pdf

Arvatz, A., Peretz, R. and Dori, Y. J. (2025), 'Self-regulated learning and reflection: a tool for teachers and students', *Metacognition and Learning*, 20, (1), 15. https://doi.org/10.1007/s11409-025-09415-3

Association for Science Education (2022), *Closing the Disadvantage Gap: Intervention Strategies from the EEF Teaching and Learning Toolkit*. https://www.ase.org.uk/sites/default/files/Closing%20the%20Disadvantage%20Gap%20%28EEF%20Toolkit%29%20ASE%20IIS.pdf

Atkins, K. and Doherty, J. (2022), 'But how and why does it "work"?: a primary school study into the impact of metacognitive strategies on disadvantaged learners', *Impact: Journal of the Chartered College of Teaching*, 14. https://my.chartered.college/impact_article/but-how-and-why-does-it-work-a-primary-school-study-into-the-impact-of-metacognitive-strategies-on-disadvantaged-learners/

Ausubel, D. P. (1968), *Educational Psychology: A Cognitive View*. New York: Holt, Rinehart & Winston.

Bandura, A. (1997), *Self-Efficacy: The Exercise of Control*. New York: W.H. Freeman.

Barrett, H. (2007), 'Researching electronic portfolios and learner engagement: the REFLECT initiative', *Journal of Adolescent & Adult Literacy*, 50, (6), 436–449.

Bernstein, B. (1971), *Class, Codes and Control, Volume 1: Theoretical Studies towards a Sociology of Language*. London: Routledge & Kegan Paul.

Bjork, E. L. and Bjork, R. A. (2011), 'Making things hard on yourself, but in a good way: creating desirable difficulties to enhance learning', in M. A. Gernsbacher, R. W. Pew, L. M. Hough and J. R. Pomerantz (eds), *Psychology and the Real World: Essays Illustrating Fundamental Contributions to Society*. New York: Worth Publishers, pp. 56–64.

Bourdieu, P. (1986), 'The forms of capital', in J. G. Richardson (ed.), *Handbook of Theory and Research for the Sociology of Education*. Westport, CT: Greenwood, pp. 241–258.

Bourdieu, P. and Passeron, J.-C. (1990), *Reproduction in Education, Society and Culture*. London: Sage Publications.

Brenner, C. A. (2022), 'Self-regulated learning, self-determination theory and teacher candidates' development of competency-based teaching practices', *Smart Learning Environments*, 9, 3.

Brookfield, S. D. (1995), *Becoming a Critically Reflective Teacher*. San Francisco: Jossey-Bass.

Brown, A. L. (1987), 'Metacognition, executive control, self-regulation, and other more mysterious mechanisms', in F. E. Weinert and R. H. Kluwe (eds), *Metacognition, Motivation, and Understanding*. Hillsdale, NJ: Erlbaum, pp. 65–116.

Cera, R., Mancini, M. and Antonietti, A. (2013), 'Relationships between metacognition, self-efficacy and self-regulation in learning', *Journal of Educational, Cultural and Psychological Studies*, 7, 115–141. https://doi.org/10.7358/ECPS-2013-007-CERA

Clarke, A. M., Morreale, S., Field, C. A., Barry, M. M. and Killackey, E. (2015), ' A systematic review of school-based interventions targeting mental health and wellbeing in adolescents', *BMC Psychology*, 3, 32. https://doi.org/10.1186/s40359-018-0242-3

Clarke, S. and Muncaster, K. (2017), *Growth Mindset Lessons: Every Child a Learner*. London: Rising Stars.

Conteh, J. (2015), *The EAL Teaching Book: Promoting Success for Multilingual Learners*. Exeter: Learning Matters.

Corno, L. (2008), 'On teaching adaptively', *Educational Psychologist*, 43, (3), 161–173.

Costello, E. J., Mustillo, S., Erkanli, A., Keeler, G. and Angold, A. (2003), 'Prevalence and development of psychiatric disorders in childhood and adolescence', *Archives of General Psychiatry*, 60, (8), 837–844. https://doi.org/10.1001/archpsyc.60.8.837

Dellar, A. (2025), 'Educational outcomes across England: examining the attainment gap in schools', Institute for Government, https://www.instituteforgovernment.org.uk/sites/default/files/2025-08/Educational-outcomes-across-england_0.pdf

Department for Education (2014), 'National curriculum in England: framework for key stages 1 to 4', www.gov.uk/government/publications/national-curriculum-in-england-framework-for-key-stages-1-to-4

Department for Education (2024a), 'Improving educational outcomes for disadvantaged children', https://publications.parliament.uk/pa/cm5901/cmselect/cmpubacc/365/report.html

Department for Education (2024b), 'Key stage 2 attainment, academic year 2023/24', https://explore-education-statistics.service.gov.uk/find-statistics/key-stage-2-attainment/2023-24

Diener, E., Oishi, S. and Tay, L. (2018), 'Advances in subjective well-being research', *Nature Human Behaviour*, 2, (4), 253–260.

Dignath, C. and Büttner, G. (2008), 'Components of fostering self-regulated learning among students: a meta-analysis on intervention studies at primary and secondary school level', *Metacognition and Learning*, 3, (3), 231–264. https://doi.org/10.1007/s11409-008-9029-x

Dignath, C. and Veenman, M. V. J. (2021), 'The role of direct strategy instruction and indirect activation of self-regulated learning — evidence from classroom observation studies', *Educational Psychology Review*, 33, (2), 489–533.

Dobson, J. and Henthorne, K. (1999), *Pupil Mobility in Schools*. London: Department for Education and Employment.

Duckworth, A. L. and Gross, J. J. (2014), 'Self-control and grit: related but separable determinants of success', *Current Directions in Psychological Science*, 23, (5), 319–325. https://doi.org/10.1177/0963721414541462

Duckworth, A. L. and Yeager, D. S. (2015), 'Measurement matters: assessing personal qualities other than cognitive ability for educational purposes', *Educational Researcher*, 44, (4), 237–251. https://doi.org/10.3102/0013189X15584327

Durlak, J. A., Weissberg, R. P., Dymnicki, A. B., Taylor, R. D. and Schellinger, K. B. (2011), 'The impact of enhancing students' social and emotional learning: a meta-analysis of school-based universal interventions', *Child Development*, 82, (1), 405–432. https://doi.org/10.1111/j.1467-8624.2010.01564.x

Dweck, C. S. (2006), *Mindset: The New Psychology of Success*. New York: Random House.

Education Endowment Foundation (EEF) (2017), 'Metacognition and self-regulated learning: guidance report', https://educationendowmentfoundation.org.uk/education-evidence/guidance-reports/metacognition-and-self-regulation

Education Endowment Foundation (EEF) (2018), 'Metacognition and self-regulated learning: guidance report', https://educationendowmentfoundation.org.uk/education-evidence/guidance-reports/metacognition-and-self-regulation

Education Endowment Foundation (EEF) (2020), 'Special educational needs in mainstream schools: guidance report', https://d2tic4wvo1iusb.cloudfront.net/production/eef-guidance-reports/send/eef_special_educational_needs_in_mainstream_schools_guidance_report_2025-04-10-110432_klxp.pdf

Education Endowment Foundation (EEF) (2025a), 'Teaching and learning toolkit', https://educationendowmentfoundation.org.uk/education-evidence/teaching-learning-toolkit

Education Endowment Foundation (EEF) (2025b), 'Updated guide to metacognition and self-regulation', https://educationendowmentfoundation.org.uk/news/updated-eef-guide-to-metacognition-and-self-regulation

Education Endowment Foundation (EEF) (2025c), 'Metacognition and self-regulated learning: guidance report', https://educationendowmentfoundation.org.uk/education-evidence/guidance-reports/metacognition

Education Endowment Foundation (EEF) (2026), 'Metacognition and self-regulated learning: guidance report', Education Endowment Foundation.

Education Endowment Foundation (EEF) (n.d.a), 'EEF blog: new EEF case studies — how metacognitive strategies can support independent learning and revision', https://educationendowmentfoundation.org.uk/news/eef-blog-new-eef-case-studies-how-metacognitive-strategies-can-support-independent-revision

Education Endowment Foundation (EEF) (n.d.b), 'Metacognition and self-regulation', EEF Teaching and Learning Toolkit, https://educationendowmentfoundation.org.uk/education-evidence/teaching-learning-toolkit/metacognition-and-self-regulation

Education Policy Institute (2024), 'Annual report 2024: disadvantage', https://epi.org.uk/publications-and-research/annual-report-2024/

Evans, G. W. and Kim, P. (2013), 'Childhood poverty, chronic stress, self-regulation, and coping', *Child Development Perspectives*, 7, (1), 43–48.

Flavell, J. H. (1979), 'Metacognition and cognitive monitoring: a new area of cognitive–developmental inquiry', *American Psychologist*, 34, (10), 906–911. https://doi.org/10.1037/0003-066X.34.10.906

Friedli, L. (2009), *Mental Health, Resilience and Inequalities*. Copenhagen: WHO Regional Office for Europe.

Frolli, A., Ricci, M. C., Rizzo, S., Di Carmine, F., Rega, A., Savarese, G. and Franzese, L. (2021), 'The effectiveness of the metacognitive model with children in disadvantaged conditions', *Clinical Psychology and Psychotherapy*, 28, (6), 1293–1306.

Gay, G. (2010), *Culturally Responsive Teaching: Theory, Research, and Practice*. New York: Teachers College Press.

Gentner, D. (1983), 'Structure-mapping: a theoretical framework for analogy', *Cognitive Science*, 7, (2), 155–170. https://doi.org/10.1016/S0364-0213(83)80009-3

Gillborn, D. (2008), *Racism and Education: Coincidence or Conspiracy?*. London: Routledge.

González, N., Moll, L. C. and Amanti, C. (eds) (2005), *Funds of Knowledge: Theorizing Practices in Households, Communities, and Classrooms*. Mahwah, NJ: Lawrence Erlbaum Associates.

Good, T. L. (2010). Teacher expectations and student achievement: self-fulfilling prophecies. In E. Baker, B. McGaw & P. Peterson (eds), International Encyclopedia of Education (3rd ed.). Oxford: Elsevier, pp. 615–621

Gorard, S. and See, B. H. (2013), *Overcoming Disadvantage in Education*. London: Routledge.

GOV.UK (n.d.), 'Children with special educational needs and disabilities (SEND)', https://www.gov.uk/children-with-special-educational-needs

Han, F. (2025), 'Sustainable lifelong learning competence: understanding university students' self-regulated learning in flipped classrooms', *Sustainability*, 17, (21), 9495. https://doi.org/10.3390/su17219495

Hart, B. and Risley, T. R. (1995), *Meaningful Differences in the Everyday Experience of Young American Children*. Baltimore, MD: Paul H. Brookes.

Hattie, J. (2009), *Visible Learning: A Synthesis of Over 800 Meta-analyses Relating to Achievement*. London: Routledge.

Hattie, J. and Donoghue, G. (2016), 'Learning strategies: a synthesis and conceptual model', *npj Science of Learning*, 1, (1), 16013. https://doi.org/10.1038/npjscilearn.2016.13

Hattie, J. and Timperley, H. (2007), 'The power of feedback', *Review of Educational Research*, 77, (1), 81–112. https://doi.org/10.3102/003465430298487

Heath, S. B. (1983), *Ways with Words: Language, Life and Work in Communities and Classrooms*. Cambridge: Cambridge University Press.

Huppert, F. A. and So, T. T. (2013), 'Flourishing across Europe: application of a new conceptual framework for defining well-being', *Social Indicators Research*, 110, (3), 837–861.

Institute for Fiscal Studies (IFS) (2020), *Inequalities in Children's Educational Attainment: The Role of Home and School Factors*. London: Institute for Fiscal Studies.

Institute for Fiscal Studies (IFS) (2024), *The State of Education: What Awaits the Next Government*. London: IFS.

Institute for Government (2025), 'Performance Tracker Local: educational outcomes', https://www.instituteforgovernment.org.uk/publication/performance-tracker-local/educational-outcomes

Jensen, E. (2009), *Teaching with Poverty in Mind: What Being Poor Does to Kids' Brains and What Schools Can Do About It*. Alexandria, VA: ASCD.

Jussim, L. and Harber, K. D. (2005), 'Teacher expectations and self-fulfilling prophecies: knowns and unknowns, resolved and unresolved controversies', *Personality and Social Psychology Review*, 9, (2), 131–155.

Karpicke, J. D. and Roediger, H. L. (2008), 'The critical importance of retrieval for learning', *Science*, 319, (5865), 966–968. https://doi.org/10.1126/science.1152408

Katz, I. and Assor, A. (2007), 'When choice motivates and when it does not', *Educational Psychology Review*, 19, (4), 429–442.

van Kesteren, M. T. R., Krabbendam, L. and Meeter, M. (2018), 'Integrating educational knowledge: reactivation of prior knowledge during educational learning enhances memory integration', *npj Science of Learning*, 3, 11. https://doi.org/10.1038/s41539-018-0027-8

Lareau, A. (2003), *Unequal Childhoods: Class, Race, and Family Life*. Berkeley, CA: University of California Press.

Lupien, S. J., McEwen, B. S., Gunnar, M. R. and Heim, C. (2009), 'Stress hormone levels and memory function in children', *Trends in Neurosciences*, 32, (9), 506–516.

Mansouri, K. (2020), *Research into Practice: Implementing Strategy and Metacognition-Based Instruction in the Teaching of EFL Listening*. Unpublished doctoral thesis. University of Reading.

McGuinness, C. (1999), *From Thinking Skills to Thinking Classrooms: A Review and Evaluation of Approaches for Developing Pupils' Thinking*. London: DfEE.

MDPI Editorial Team (2025), 'The interplay of self-regulated learning and academic emotion regulation: implications for student resilience', *Education Sciences*, 15, (7), 804. https://www.mdpi.com/2227-7102/15/7/804

Mercer, N. and Littleton, K. (2007), *Dialogue and the Development of Children's Thinking: A Sociocultural Approach*. London: Routledge.

Moffitt, T. E., Arseneault, L., Belsky, D., Dickson, N., Hancox, R. J., Harrington, H. L., Houts, R., Poulton, R., Roberts, B. W., Ross, S., Sears, M. R., Thomson, W. M. and Caspi, A. (2011), 'A gradient of childhood self-control predicts health, wealth, and public safety', *Proceedings of the National Academy of Sciences*, 108, (7), 2693–2698. https://doi.org/10.1073/pnas.1010076108

Mughal, A. (2021), *Think!: Metacognition-Powered Primary Teaching*. London: Corwin Press.

Muijs, D. and Bokhove, C. (2020), *Metacognition and Self-Regulation: Evidence Review*. London: Education Endowment Foundation.

Norman, E., Pfuhl, G. and Artelt, C. (2023), 'Associations between metacognition, mindfulness, experiential avoidance, depression, and anxiety', *BMC Psychology*, 11, (1), 139.

Panadero, E. (2017), 'A review of self-regulated learning: six models and four directions for research', *Frontiers in Psychology*, 8, Article 422. https://doi.org/10.3389/fpsyg.2017.00422

Paris, A. H. and Paris, S. G. (2003), 'Assessing narrative comprehension in young children', *Reading Research Quarterly*, 38, (1), 36–76. https://doi.org/10.1598/RRQ.38.1.3

Perry, B. D. and Szalavitz, M. (2006), *The Boy Who Was Raised as a Dog: And Other Stories from a Child Psychiatrist's Notebook*. New York: Basic Books.

Pinnacle Learning Research School (2025), 'Empowering disadvantaged learners: how the EEF's seven steps build independent, focused students', Research Schools Network.

Pressley, M. and Afflerbach, P. (1995), *Verbal Protocols of Reading: The Nature of Constructively Responsive Reading*. Hillsdale, NJ: Lawrence Erlbaum Associates.

Quigley, A., Muijs, D. and Stringer, E. (2018), *Metacognition and Self-Regulated Learning: Guidance Report*. London: Education Endowment Foundation. https://educationendowmentfoundation.org.uk/education-evidence/guidance-reports/metacognition

Reiss, F. (2013), 'Socioeconomic inequalities and mental health problems in children and adolescents: a systematic review', *Social Science & Medicine*, 90, 24–31.

Research Schools Network (2023), 'Empowering disadvantaged learners: how the EEF's seven steps build independent, focused students', https://researchschool.org.uk/pinnacle-learning/news/empowering-disadvantaged-learners-how-the-eefs-seven-steps-build-independent-focused-students (Accessed: 10 March 2026).

Robinson, D. et al. (2024), 'Annual report 2024: SEND', Education Policy Institute, 15 July. https://epi.org.uk/annual-report-2024-send-2/

Roffey, S. (2012), 'Pupil wellbeing – teacher wellbeing: two sides of the same coin?', *Educational and Child Psychology*, 29, (4), 8–17.

Rosenthal, R. and Jacobson, L. (1968), *Pygmalion in the Classroom: Teacher Expectation and Pupils' Intellectual Development*. New York: Holt, Rinehart & Winston.

Rubie-Davies, C. M. and Hattie, J. A. (2024), 'The powerful impact of teacher expectations: a narrative review', *Journal of the Royal Society of New Zealand*, 55, (2), 343–371. https://www.tandfonline.com/doi/pdf/10.1080/03036758.2024.2393296

Ryff, C. D. (1989), 'Happiness is everything, or is it? Explorations on the meaning of psychological well-being', *Journal of Personality and Social Psychology*, 57, (6), 1069–1081.

Schoenfeld, A. H. (1985), *Mathematical Problem Solving*. Orlando, FL: Academic Press.

Schonert-Reichl, K. A. and Roeser, R. W. (2016), 'Social and emotional learning and teachers', in J. A. Durlak, C. E. Domitrovich, R. P. Weissberg and T. P. Gulotta (eds), *Handbook of Social and Emotional Learning: Research and Practice*. New York: The Guilford Press, pp. 137–152.

Schraw, G. and Dennison, R. S. (1994), 'Assessing metacognitive awareness', *Contemporary Educational Psychology*, 19, (4), 460–475.

Seligman, M. E. P. (1972), 'Learned helplessness', *Annual Review of Medicine*, 23, (1), 407–412.

Simón-Grábalos, D. et al. (2025), 'Systematic review on self-regulated learning training programs'.

Sirin, S. R. (2005), 'Socioeconomic status and academic achievement: a meta-analytic review of research', *Review of Educational Research*, 75, (3), 417–453.

Strand, S. (2014), 'Ethnicity, gender, social class and achievement gaps at age 16: intersectionality and "getting it" for the white working class', *Research Papers in Education*, 29, (2), 131–171.

Strand, S. and Demie, F. (2006), 'English language acquisition and attainment in secondary schools', *Educational Studies*, 32, (2), 215–231. https://doi.org/10.1080/03055690600631119

Sultana, F., Watkins, R. C., Baghal, T. A. and Hughes, J. C. (2025), 'An evaluation of secondary school students' use and understanding of learning strategies to study and revise for science examinations', *Education Sciences*, 15, (1), 101. https://www.mdpi.com/2227-7102/15/1/101

Sutton Trust (2010), *The Educational Backgrounds of Leading Lawyers, Journalists, Vice Chancellors, Politicians, Medics and Chief Executives*. London: Sutton Trust.

Sutton Trust (2019), *Social Mobility and Educational Gaps*. London: Sutton Trust.

Sutton Trust (2021), *COVID-19 and Education: The Widening Gap in Disadvantaged Pupils' Learning*. London: Sutton Trust.

Sylva, K., Melhuish, E., Sammons, P., Siraj-Blatchford, I. and Taggart, B. (2004), *The Effective Provision of Pre-School Education (EPPE) Project: Final Report:*

A Longitudinal Study Funded by the DfES 1997–2004. London: Institute of Education, University of London/Department for Education and Skills/Sure Start. https://discovery.ucl.ac.uk/id/eprint/10005309

Taylor, R., Oberle, E., Durlak, J. A. and Weissberg, R. P. (2017), 'Promoting positive youth development through school-based social and emotional learning interventions: a meta-analysis of follow-up effects', *Child Development*, 88, (4), 1156–1171. https://doi.org/10.1111/cdev.12864

Trivedi, H. and Harrison, N. (2022), *Attachment Aware and Trauma-Informed Schools Programmes: Positive Practice Examples from Local Authorities*. Rees Centre, Department of Education, University of Oxford and The Hadley Trust. https://www.education.ox.ac.uk/wp-content/uploads/2022/07/Hadleys-AATI-Report.pdf

Veenman, M. V. J., Van Hout-Wolters, B. H. A. M. and Afflerbach, P. (2006), 'Metacognition and learning: conceptual and methodological considerations', *Metacognition and Learning*, 1, (1), 1–14.

Vygotsky, L. S. (1978), *Mind in Society: The Development of Higher Psychological Processes*. Cambridge, MA: Harvard University Press.

Wang, M. C., Haertel, G. D. and Walberg, H. J. (1990), 'What influences learning? A content analysis of review literature', *Journal of Educational Research*, 84, (1), 30–43. https://doi.org/10.1080/00220671.1990.10885988

Winne, P. H. and Azevedo, R. (2022), 'Metacognition and self-regulated learning', in R. K. Sawyer (ed.), *The Cambridge Handbook of the Learning Sciences* (3rd edn). Cambridge: Cambridge University Press, pp. 93–113.

World Health Organization (WHO) (2013), *Mental Health Action Plan 2013–2020*. Geneva: WHO.

Xu, L., Duan, P., Padua, S. A. and Li, C. (2022), 'The impact of self-regulated learning strategies on academic performance for online learning during COVID-19', *Frontiers in Psychology*, 13, 1047680. https://doi.org/10.3389/fpsyg.2022.1047680

Yeager, D. S. and Dweck, C. S. (2012), 'Mindsets that promote resilience: when students believe that personal characteristics can be developed', *Educational Psychologist*, 47, (4), 302–314.

Youssef, N. H. and Alibraheim, E. A. (2025), 'Self-regulated learning strategies among graduate students and their relationship with statistics anxiety', *Education Sciences*, 15, (1), 17. https://doi.org/10.3390/educsci15010017

Zhang, W., Zhang, D. and Zhang, L. J. (2021), 'Metacognitive instruction for sustainable learning', *Sustainability*, 13, (11), 6275. https://doi.org/10.3390/su13116275

Zimmerman, B. J. (2002), 'Becoming a self-regulated learner: an overview', *Theory into Practice*, 41, (2), 64–70. https://doi.org/10.1207/s15430421tip4102_2

Zimmerman, B. J. and Risemberg, R. (1997), 'Self-regulatory dimensions of academic learning and motivation', in G. D. Phye (ed.), *Handbook of Academic Learning: Construction of Knowledge*. San Diego: Academic Press, pp. 105–125. https://doi.org/10.1016/B978-012554255-5/50005-3

Index